# The great omission

# The great omission

A call to restore 'mission'
to the heart of the local church

Trevor Harris

 EVANGELICAL PRESS

EVANGELICAL PRESS
Faverdale North Industrial Estate, Darlington, DL3 0PH,
England

Evangelical Press USA
P. O. Box 825, Webster, New York 14580, USA

e-mail: sales@evangelicalpress.org
web: www.evangelicalpress.org

First published 2005

British Library Cataloguing in Publication Data available

ISBN 0 85234 583 6

Printed and bound in Great Britain by Creative Print and
Design Wales, Ebbw Vale, South Wales.

*To my former colleagues
in Slavic Gospel Association
with whom it was my joy to serve
through thirty years of privileged ministry.*

# Contents

# Preface

In the course of ministry with Slavic Gospel Association, particularly over the last few years, and in talking with pastors and church leaders across the UK, I have sensed an increasing frustration concerning the whole issue of 'mission' and the local church.

Many churches that are seeing encouraging growth and blessing appear to have a problem in recognizing that Christ's mandate to the church is not only local, but also global. Conversely, those who feel they are in 'the day of small things' here in the UK find it far easier to isolate their thinking on 'mission' to overseas ministry. In either case, one can only be drawn to the conclusion that true 'mission', in its broadest sense, has somehow been sidelined and marginalized, rather than having its intended place as the 'heartbeat' of the church. If the chapters that follow cause the reader to prayerfully and realistically reassess the place of mission in the local church, they will have accomplished their aim.

In contrast to the UK scene, it has been a privilege to witness the way in which the church in Eastern Europe has 'missioned' the gospel so effectively through local church life, not only during the repressive days of Communism, but also with the subsequent freedoms that came following the remarkable changes of 1989, typified by the fall of the Berlin Wall. It is with these concerns and from these experiences that this book has come into being. In essence, most of the 'theology of mission' that follows is the basis of Bible teaching that has been given over the years in the mission schools within Eastern Europe with which S.G.A. is associated. Therefore much of the illustrative material is drawn from this background, trusting that it will not only challenge but also encourage us all in this great and privileged calling of proclaiming Christ, both at home and abroad.

Appreciation must be expressed to Rev. Bill Patterson for his encouragement to put these things into writing. Also to Pauline Francis who willingly volunteered to proof-read the initial draft. Then to my wife Joan who, from her experience of Eastern Europe too, frequently and patiently found herself acting as a 'sounding board', as the book evolved.

Trevor Harris

# 1.
# Another step
# down a well-worn pathway!

My thirty years of ministry in Central and Eastern Europe with Slavic Gospel Association gave me a God-given privilege to witness personally the remarkable events in history which have shaped today's map of Europe. As the never-to-be-forgotten momentous year of 1989 heralded the tearing down of the notorious Berlin Wall and all it stood for, so the rapid domino effect that occurred across Eastern Europe opened the former countries of the Communist Eastern Bloc to the gospel, in a manner that had not been possible for decades.

December 1989 saw us involved in another Bible-teaching visit to Romania. Entry into the country had brought with it another intense scrutiny by the 'Securitate'. Over the years we had come to know this as part of the inevitable frontier controls. Thankfully the Lord answered prayer yet again and after almost three hours of attention and questioning, our passports were returned and we were allowed entry. During the visit we were followed and monitored as usual and great care had to be exercised in order to avoid bringing more pressures on the Romanian believers than they were already experiencing. Now, with the ministry completed, it was time to leave Romania and make the long wintery drive home, in anticipation of the Christmas celebrations with our own family and friends. Although various countries of Eastern Europe were undergoing a traumatic change, the Romanian regime seemed unshakable.

The heavy-handed dictatorship appeared to be as severe as ever. This impression was heightened by the fact that whilst in Romania, the bloodless 'Velvet Revolution' in Czechoslovakia had taken place. In fact the westward drive around the Vienna orbital motorway was a fascinating experience. To our amazement every other car was Czech, interspersed with Czech buses, all making their way into the centre of Vienna. The Czech border was open and hundreds were visiting the city for their first taste of 'the West'.

As the Christmas season began to unfold, 17 December brought startling news of a 'Romanian revolution'. The unthinkable was happening and by Christmas Day the dictatorship was dealt with by a firing squad. Unlike Czechoslovakia, many Romanian lives were lost as the populace was caught in the crossfire of revolution.

This was probably the most difficult Christmas we had ever experienced. As we sat glued to both television and radio reports, the numerous attempts to telephone our Christian brothers and sisters in Romania proved fruitless. The frontier was closed and all landline telephone communication cut, and of course these were days when mobile telephones and electronic mail were unknown in Eastern Europe. We had many thoughts and questions intermingled with our prayers. What of all our friends? How had the revolution affected them and the churches in which they worshipped? — and there was much more beside.

By Friday 5 January 1990 I was sitting on the Romanian border once again. The frontiers had just opened and the officials were affable and friendly. The same personnel who had harassed us over the years now welcomed us. Hands were shaking ours and giving us every assistance to speed our entry. When asked, 'What is in your vehicle?' we answered, 'Practical help and Romanian Bibles.' 'That's good,' said the officer with a smile. Unbelievably we heard him saying, 'Thank you for coming to the "new" Romania — thank you for helping us.'

What made this even more remarkable was that these words came from a man who had given us so many problems on previous occasions. Such was the atmosphere that, at the suggestion of a photograph, he adjusted his cap and the tricolour ribbon of the revolution displayed on his arm, and straightening his tie he said, 'Why not!' That was a momentous visit. All our Christian friends were found to be safe and there were many tears as they shared how the Lord had overshadowed and protected them.

Almost overnight unprecedented opportunities for work and witness presented themselves to the national Christians of these countries and with enthusiasm and dedication they grasped them with both hands. Yes, on occasions the Eastern European believers had to learn the hard way, and in particular, that not everything offered by 'western evangelicalism' was always beneficial. However, as those of us from the West looked on, it was obvious that this was not a mere passing euphoria brought about by newly-found freedoms, but rather a deep and consuming desire to bring the good news of salvation through Jesus Christ to their own peoples. How can one ever forget hearing Romanian Christians praying in 1981 that in their lifetime they would see the day when they could print Bibles openly, preach the gospel from every street corner in their city and plant new local churches in the surrounding villages? Remember, these were days when the dictator Nicolae Ceausescu and his wife Elena held Romania in an iron fist, part of which was to suppress the church with harsh and even brutal measures. From a human point of view, what the believers were praying for was impossible, but they would not be deterred.

During one visit to an Eastern European pastor in the early 1980s, we were talking over the challenges of ministry in a Communist-controlled society when he suddenly interjected with this statement, 'Brother Trevor, I have a big problem with my young people!' I wondered what was coming next, knowing how many pastors had expressed exactly that sentiment on more than one occasion. He continued: 'The problem is that I am having to hold them back from evangelizing openly on the streets. You know how it is; if they did this our church would be closed down by the authorities.' I could not help thinking how many pastors in the West would just long to have a problem like that.

Certainly the subsequent overall, numerical and spiritual growth of the church in Central and Eastern Europe since the fall of Communism brings its own challenge. For example, the Evangelical Congregationalists of Bulgaria almost trebled their number of local congregations in the decade that followed the 1989 revolution. Similarly, in that same period, a local Baptist church in central Romania saw eleven new churches planted in the villages surrounding their town. Many other examples could be given, but, above all, the undeniable fact is that God graciously blessed national Christians who were serious about 'mission' and who were prepared to pay the cost of obedient surrender of their lives to God's Word.

Long before the openness came, one Eastern European pastor with whom I was in contact saw the need for trained leadership. He knew all too well that this was one of the main areas targeted for annihilation by the Communist regime. Consequently he had been engaged in unofficial training programmes even prior to 1989. With the new freedoms, it became possible to formalize and enhance Bible training, and the pastor's careful forethought had already produced some who were able to take responsibility for the work of the gospel.

With the newly-found openness came the time to begin training many others. As part of this, he could take the students away for a few days of retreat, for fellowship and study together, without fear of the prying eyes of the secret police. On one such occasion the group camped in a beautiful mountainous region of their country and as the days progressed a few people from the nearby village came to enquire who they were. Through this, contact was made with the village, culminating in the group hiring the local hall for an evangelistic meeting. The hall had never seen such a crowd, as it overflowed with people from the village, and that Friday evening saw a number responding to the challenge and call of the gospel.

On Saturday and Sunday morning the new converts eagerly joined the group studying the Scriptures. They rejoiced in the faithfulness of God, until one of the villagers noticed that the tents were being taken down, as the group prepared to leave and drive the 150 kilometre return journey to their home city. His response was, 'What is to happen to us? We have no other Christians with whom to meet and no church to attend.'

Suddenly the pastor and his group were brought to earth with a bump. What was to happen to these 'babes' in Christ? The pastor made this promise: 'Give us one week and we will be in contact with you again.' Back in their home city the pastor gathered the group together on the Monday evening to ask one simple question: 'Who will go?' The silence that followed was marked with serious expressions on every face, as each one considered the implications of such a question. One of the group said, 'Let's pray', and as they bowed their heads in prayer there was a further time of awesome silence before anyone could find the words to pray audibly. As the time of prayer came to an end one brother said, 'I will go.'

He had no car and was all too aware that the 150 kilometres would mean taking a train, then a bus and trekking the final five kilometres on foot. However, he did this every weekend for almost a year. In the beginning the pleasant autumnal weather made the two-way journey quite agreeable, but as the seasons changed he soon found himself having to walk through deep winter snows. It was not easy, but by God's grace he persevered. The little congregation began to outgrow the home in which they met and God blessed them in a wonderful way.

Five years later that village church not only had fifty members meeting in their own church building, but they had also planted two other local churches in nearby villages. As the pastor commented: 'See what happens when a man catches the heartbeat of God and is prepared to pay the price.'

In contrast, it seems to be acknowledged that, in general terms at least, today's UK scene is far removed from this. In traversing the country, one gains an overwhelming impression that the 'Great Commission' so clearly given in the Scriptures to the church of Jesus Christ of every age has somehow become marginalized. It seems that rather than being the church's lifeblood, at best 'mission' has been put on the periphery of its vision and thinking. Like most things, this has not happened suddenly. Over the last thirty years other writers have made similar observations. For example, as far back as 1976 Martin Goldsmith was writing of a basic weakness he observed, with these comments:

*throughout our churches and Christian Unions world-wide mission appears to be an optional extra to be indulged in by those who are spiritually keen and who happen to be interested in it. Furthermore, those who try to stimulate a belief that world mission is an integral part of the life of the church find that such exhortations fail to make much impact.*[1]

Certainly not all can be laid at the door of the local church. Often mission agencies have failed to present what God is doing in his harvest field in a relevant and effective manner. However, perhaps part of the problem is that our churches are failing to teach worldwide mission as a basic theme of the whole Bible. How often do we find mission being presented as if it hinged on a few isolated verses of Scripture?

However, having made that comment, it is still beneficial to begin with one such passage. Therefore let us pause here for a moment to be reminded of that Great Commission given by the Lord Jesus as recorded in the Gospel of Matthew, chapter 28, verses 16-20:

Now the eleven disciples went to Galilee, to the mountain to which Jesus had directed and made appointment with them. And when they saw Him, they fell down and worshipped Him; but some doubted. Jesus approached and, breaking the silence, said to them, All authority [all power of rule] in heaven and on earth has been given to Me. Go then and make disciples of all the nations, baptizing them into the name of the Father and of the Son and of the Holy Spirit, teaching them to observe everything that I have commanded you, and behold, I am with you all the days [perpetually, uniformly, and on every occasion] to the [very] close and consummation of the age. Amen [so let it be]

(Amplified New Testament).

In contrast to this injunction of Scripture, John Millar of Pennsylvania aptly coined the phrase 'The Ingrown Church'[2] with the suggestion that the 'self-centred ethos' which pervades our society has become a common phenomenon and the 'norm' for the majority of our contemporary evangelical churches. A counter argument could be made against the validity of such an assessment, particularly in the light of the 'church-growth' emphasis of the last decade, but it is increasingly evident that church growth centred on popularized man-made solutions, rather than biblical truth based on faith in God's mercy and grace, is ultimately a dangerous and doomed creation. Maybe A. W. Tozer puts his finger on the root problem, in drawing our attention to the Gospel of John chapter 3 verse 17 (AV):

> For God sent not his Son into the world to condemn the world; but that the world through him might be saved.

As only Tozer can, he proposes that this is a 'proclamation extraordinary'[3] from the living God and then asks:

> *Why then, among professing Christians in our churches, is there a blank kind of indifference and an incredible apathy to such an extraordinary proclamation of God's best intentions for us. With this gravely significant message from the heart of God Himself, why are we so indifferent? Why, upon our eyes seems to have fallen a strange dimness, to our ears a strange dullness, in our minds a stupor and in our hearts a great callousness.*

As the apostle John records this statement from the lips of Jesus in John 3:17, its understanding in the mind of the Jewish hearer would have been almost incomprehensible. For the Jew, the Messiah at his coming would condemn the heathen.

It would be unbelievable that God's redemptive purpose was not confined to the Jews but embraced 'the world'. Add to this that the primary objective of Christ's first coming was not to condemn but to save, and this charged the church's responsibility and privilege with a completely new concept. It is not insignificant that of the four different words used in the Scriptures and translated as 'the world', in John's Gospel chapter 1, verses 10-11, speaking of Jesus coming 'into the world', and here in chapter 3:17, the force of the original text points us to the particular and specific meaning of 'the world' as 'the sum total of humanity in the world — people of every tribe and nation of every generation'. So as Christ came to proffer salvation to the sum total of humanity in the world, so the followers of Christ are commissioned to go into 'all the world' (Mark 16:15) and make disciples of all nations (Matthew 28:19).

In a recent conversation on the subject of mission concern, with the pastor of what would be considered a thriving evangelical church in the UK, I was both encouraged and surprised by his comments. He told how his church gave 60% of their offerings to 'mission'. In fact, he said, the people here will give for 'mission' until their pockets bleed. He went on to speak of the church's active 'Mission Board' and its regular exposure to 'missions' through midweek meetings. Then his voice changed and with deep concern he said that although all this was so encouraging, something was drastically amiss, because they were not seeing those who were prepared to 'go'.

Shortly after this I was invited to attend a conference which drew together pastors and church leaders from many parts of the UK. The lunchtime break afforded a good opportunity to browse in the fairly extensive bookshop, which had been brought in for the duration of the conference. Although there were many fine books on display, sadly, the great omission was patently obvious with not one title associated with, or relating to, the subject of 'mission'.

So it is that I humbly submit these writings for serious and prayerful consideration. In the following chapters we will simply attempt to come from a biblical basis, to understand what mission is and how today's church in the UK can take stock of its approach to the Great Commission, which was given by the one whom the church claims to be its Lord and Saviour.

The manner in which we spend our lives will always revolve around our devotion to Christ. Unless there is a deep sense of personal indebtedness to the Saviour, born out of some understanding of the great cost of our redemption, it is unlikely that we will have a lasting or influential concern for 'mission'.

Count Zinzendorf, at a critical point in his spiritual experience, was deeply moved as he gazed at Steinberg's picture of the crucifixion in the Dusseldorf Art Gallery. The painting carried the inscription:

All this I did for thee, what hast thou done for Me?

This came as a direct and personal challenge to Zinzendorf and that day the vision of Christ's dying love transformed his life. 'I have', he exclaimed, 'but one passion — 'tis He, and only He.'

Today we recall that it was largely due to the inspiration of Zinzendorf's leadership that the Moravian church became such a potent force in world evangelization.

# 2.
# The what, whys & wherefores!

The *Mission Impossible* films portray a group of special agents who worked to right the wrongs of those who attempted to put themselves outside the law. This was their mission in life. We use the phrase, 'a man with a mission', but what do we mean when we use that all-embracing word — 'mission'? The dictionary definition gives a variety of possibilities varying from 'a military task' to 'a permanent overseas embassy' or 'an organized missionary work, to increase church membership or propagate a religious faith, usually conducted overseas'. The history of the church in relation to mission shows a great diversity in both understanding what this actually means and in what is its motivation and practice. If nothing else, this reminds us that in considering the subject, it will be helpful to attempt to define our terminology.

## Setting the parameters

Maybe some of the following comments will assist us in determining important characteristics of the biblical concept of 'mission'.

*Mission embraces everything which God has sent His people into the world to do. Not only what He commands His people to do, but everything He sends His people to do.*

(Dr John Stott)

*…just as a fire cannot give out its warmth without burning, so with the Christian Church, where mission is its life and cause.*

(Emil Brunner)

*Mission is the Church of Jesus Christ turning itself inside-out.*

(Anon.)

*To be a Christian is to be a member of a missionary community and to participate in the activity of a missionary God.*

(Daniel Niles)

*Every Christian is either a missionary or an imposter.*

(C. H. Spurgeon)

In drawing some of these thoughts together we begin to pick up important pointers regarding the true meaning of mission in its biblical sense. As we will see later, mission is not of human conception or undertaking, invented by the church. Mission did not begin with the disciples, the apostle Paul or William Carey, who is often called the 'Father of Modern Missions'. Its source is God himself; it is directed by him into the world, as he sends his church to engage in this privileged and awesome task of communicating a message of redemption to a lost world. Consequently, since the church consists of every true disciple of Jesus Christ, all are to be part of this great activity.

Peskott and Ramachandra make this point most forcibly from the Old Testament when they offer the following comment:

*the book of Deuteronomy is largely Moses' exhortation to Israel to remember the words of Yahweh, both for their own well-being and that they might be a light to the nations.*[1]

The supreme revelation of this truth is in Jesus Christ, sent by the Father to a lost world as an expression of God's heart of love and mercy. Following this we see Jesus sending out all the twelve disciples (Matthew 10:5), finally culminating in the Saviour's words to them as recorded in John's Gospel chapter 20:21: 'As the Father has sent me, I am sending you.' And then the Father and the Son send the Holy Spirit to equip and empower the disciples. So we begin to see that, with regard to mission, the 'sending concept' is evident as a core truth.

Matthew 9:38 is yet another one of those much quoted 'missionary texts':

So pray to the Lord of the harvest to force out and thrust labourers into His harvest

(Amplified New Testament).

Here the force of the original text is that the 'sending out' is a violent flinging out of labourers, for that is often what it takes for God to move our cold and unresponsive hearts. But more importantly, notice the context, where Jesus is going into the cities and villages, teaching and preaching the gospel of the kingdom and healing the sick (v. 35), and as he sees the multitudes harassed and scattered, like sheep without a shepherd, we read (v. 37):

Then he said to his disciples, 'The harvest is plentiful...
Ask the Lord of the harvest, therefore, to send out workers into his harvest field.'

This is no isolated text but an integral part of the whole of our Lord's ministry and again, as we shall endeavour to see later, the whole of the Bible, as the Word of God, has this missionary character. It is said that this is the great difference between the Bible and other 'sacred' books. Whereas the latter record man's search for God, the Bible reveals God's gracious and merciful search for man.

> For God so greatly loved and dearly prized the world that He (even) gave up His only [unique] begotten Son, so that whoever believes in [trusts in, clings to, relies on] Him shall not perish [come to destruction, be lost] but have eternal [everlasting] life
>
> (John 3:16, Amplified New Testament).

## Jesus and the Great Commission

In looking at the words and teaching of Christ to his followers in the latter part of his earthly ministry and following his resurrection, his emphasis becomes so obvious. The one thing that is recorded in the Scriptures, not once but on five occasions, is 'the Great Commission'.

> 'All authority in heaven and on earth has been given to me. Therefore go and make disciples of all nations… And surely I am with you always, to the very end of the age'
>
> (Matthew 28:18-20).

> 'Go into all the world and preach the good news to all creation'
>
> (Mark 16:15).

'...and repentance and forgiveness of sins will be preached in his name to all nations, beginning at Jerusalem. You are witnesses of these things'

(Luke 24:47-48).

John 20:21 records Christ as saying to his disciples:

'As the Father has sent me, I am sending you.'

In Acts 1:8 Jesus cuts across the irrelevances of the disciples' discussion on the 'times & seasons' to state:

'But you will receive power when the Holy Spirit comes on you; and you will be my witnesses in Jerusalem, and in all Judea and Samaria, and to the ends of the earth.'

Notice how under the Spirit of God each writer is bringing a different focus on Christ's words. Like a precious diamond being turned so that its different facets catch the light and show another aspect of its beauty, so it is with the Gospel writers concerning Christ and his words. As Matthew, the Jew of Jews, points us to Christ the Messiah King so he emphasizes the power invested in the one who gives this Great Commission. Mark is probably writing to non-Christian Romans when he presents Christ as the Servant Redeemer and so he highlights a gospel for the entire world and for every creature.

In his record of the Great Commission, Dr Luke brings us to Christ the compassionate Son of Man through whom forgiveness of sins will be given to all who repent. John, as 'the disciple whom Jesus loved', writes of Christ the Son of God, with whom he can have such an intimate relationship, even to the extent of being commissioned personally by his Saviour and Lord. Finally, as Dr Luke pens the Acts record of 1:8 he gives us, with clinical detail, God's strategy for implementing the Great Commission.

The point is that this was not a matter of the apostolic church considering mission as a secondary affair, or even of equal importance along with other matters; it was the supreme objective to which all else was to be subservient.

This then begs the question, why did Christ make this emphasis and the Spirit of God prompt the Gospel writers to write in this way? What is the purpose of the Great Commission? Could it be that this is the overriding and urgent question which the church of Jesus Christ in the UK must answer today, in order to regain its perspective and purpose for tomorrow?

Around 1990 when the USSR was collapsing, Russian troops were quickly withdrawn from the dominantly rural and impoverished Soviet Republic of Moldova. Not to be confused with Moldavia (which is Romania's eastern province), the little Republic of Moldova is 'sandwiched' between Romania and the Ukraine and gained its independence in 1991. The mix of six ethnic groups soon brought problems and in 1992 fighting ensued in eastern Moldova.

In the decade that followed, an economic assessment of all the European countries placed Moldova at the bottom of the league table. Nevertheless a gospel witness was already well established and even in the days of Communist rule, the evangelical church was very active. It was here that one of the 'underground' printing presses produced Bibles in the Russian language, the discovery of which led to the long-term imprisonment of a number of Christians. As the openness came, that kind of fervour among the evangelical believers brought about a remarkable church-planting programme, which is ongoing today.

The country was divided into seven areas and as nationals are trained, each area is being systematically reached with the gospel. Not content with this, the Moldovan evangelical church has been sending missionaries as far as the northern extremes of Siberia. As we thank God for giving the Moldovan believers such vision and concern for the spread of the gospel, surely here, at least, is a clue to the reason behind the Great Commission? Namely, a passion for the lost!

That great missionary pioneer Hudson Taylor testified that he would never have thought of becoming a missionary, but for his deep conviction of the lost condition of the 'heathen' and their utter need of Christ. Could there be any more important motivation than this to cause each follower of Christ to give themselves to mission?

However, I suggest that even this motive calls for caution. The problem with setting the salvation of the lost or the multiplication of local churches as the prime objective for mission advocates a theology that makes the church an end in itself to God's mission. Orlando Costas asks in his writings on the church and mission:

*Isn't the Gospel the good news of the kingdom? Who is the centre of the kingdom − Christ or the Church?*[2]

In the work of the gospel there is always a danger that we get so caught up in the details of what we are doing that we forget why we are doing it, even to the extent of earnestly and sincerely seeking to bring the good news of salvation to the lost.

## Immediate and ultimate goals

A helpful passage of Scripture is 1 Corinthians 15:24-28:

> Then the end will come, when he [Christ] hands over
> the kingdom to God the Father after he has destroyed all
> dominion, authority and power. For he must reign until
> he has put all his enemies under his feet. The last enemy
> to be destroyed is death. For he 'has put everything under
> his feet' [quoting from Psalm 8:6]. Now when it says that
> 'everything' has been put under him, it is clear that this
> does not include God himself, who put everything under
> Christ. When he has done this, then the Son himself will
> be made subject to him who put everything under him
> [Christ], so that God may be all in all.

The context of 1 Corinthians 15 is that of the risen Christ
who is the centre of the believer's faith and the passage follows
this sequence:

- The Saviour, having risen from the dead, has a delegated
  royalty to rule over his kingdom;
- This mediatorial kingdom will come to an end when all the
  opposing power is put down (vv. 24-25);
- The delegated royalty will then be delivered back to the
  Father by the Son (v. 28);
- That God will be all in all (v. 28).

This passage gives us the 'ultimate goal' of the Great
Commission, namely that 'God might be all in all', with the
'immediate goal' as the exercise of Christ's righteous and loving
reign known in the lives of sinful mankind.

In teaching this subject over a number of years I have frequently posed the question, 'What do you see as the purpose of the Great Commission?' Inevitably this has produced a variety of responses. Some would say, 'to see precious souls being saved' or 'to establish as many Bible-preaching churches as possible'. Others have said, 'to Christianize the whole world and so transform individual societies and nations'. Yet others have offered, 'to hasten Christ's return'. I believe this latter thought must be taken with great care, since the church ought to avoid the danger of imagining that its share in God's mission preconditions the final fulfilment of Christ's promised return.

However, we see all these comments as worthy and sincere reasons for the church of Jesus Christ desiring to align itself with God's purpose and intent for a lost and sinful world that is under his righteous judgement. Nevertheless, I believe we are seeing here that these stated activities and ministries are but mere channels through which that immediate goal is to be reached — that Christ's reign will be known and acknowledged — so that, finally, the ultimate goal will be established — that God is all in all.

Certainly the church's task is never finished until Christ's return. One of the proofs of the reality of the nineteenth-century revival in England was that those who rejoiced in what was accomplished saw an unfinished worldwide task and overseas mission was born. Today, it is estimated that over two thousand million people still have no church in their own culture through which Christ is being taught and revealed. Considering the decade that followed the fall of Communism in the former Soviet Union and Eastern Europe, if all the towns, cities and villages were put together within that landmass, only one in ten could claim to have a Bible-preaching local church within its community. Although disputed by some church-growth statistics, there is reasonable evidence to suggest that although there are more Christians living on the earth today than ever before in the history of the world, in terms of the world's total population, the numerical percentage of Christians is reducing. The New Testament clearly holds a balance and tension between passages teaching that the kingdom of God has come in the person of Christ, with that of the kingdom as a future culmination of God's work of grace. In the parables Christ taught of a growing kingdom, as illustrated in the seed that grows into a tree or the quiet working of the leaven in bread. Jesus said, 'the kingdom of God is within you' — within the church. This implies that, potentially, the kingdom can be further established and extended.

Probably the most urgent and vital 'missionary prayer' we can ever pray is 'Your kingdom come, your will be done on earth as it is in heaven' (Matthew 6:10).

# 3.
# Back to basics

The autumn of 1992 heralded the long-awaited visit to the UK of the 'Bethany Choir' from Romania — a choir consisting of thirty-two ordinary Romanian young people who, having found a personal and living faith in Jesus Christ, were eager to share their testimony in word and song with all who would gather to meet them. Among them were students, engineers, a nurse, a blacksmith, a bookkeeper, a taxi driver, housewives and factory workers. Above all, the Slavic Gospel Association wanted to give them a 'mission platform' through which to make an impact with the gospel throughout the UK and it was certainly some 'platform'. The tour consisted of seventeen major city venues throughout England, Wales, Scotland and Northern Ireland in twenty-one days.

I had first come to know these young people in 'unofficial' Bible-teaching sessions in Romania before the 1989 collapse of Communism. Here was a group of young people who were not simply serious about their music, but also about getting to know God's Word in order to serve him through their local congregation. Their pastor had attended similar teaching sessions with us in previous years and this was how the invitation came to minister to his young people. In fact it was not until a birthday occurred during one of the Bible teaching days that I realized that the majority of the study group formed the choir in the church. Suddenly, during the morning break, this glorious and rich harmony filled the room as the group sang the Romanian equivalent of 'happy birthday' to the birthday girl.

The openness that followed 1989 gave an opportunity for the choir to travel to the UK and members of the Slavic Gospel Association team committed a great deal of time in prayer and effort to arrange the tour. The Lord's presence was known night by night and he graciously blessed the musical programme, which included personal testimonies prior to their pastor's closing epilogue. I will never forget the evening when Georgiana shared how she came to saving faith. This quiet unassuming girl in her early twenties told of the great struggle that went on in her soul for over twelve months before she finally came to the cross of Christ. In her attractive accented English she said, 'My "borning again" was not easy, but God was so gracious and patient with me. How wonderful to know the forgiveness of sins and to belong to Jesus Christ! What a privilege to be called of God to follow and serve the Saviour!' Georgiana's words summed up what I witnessed among the group in those three hectic weeks of travel and meetings. They had this wonderful sense and understanding of the privilege and joy that was theirs in being called to serve their Lord and Master.

It seems to me that this is an area where we have denigrated the whole concept of service for God and the missionary call. Many of our missionary appeals almost seem to give the impression that we ought to engage in these things because God needs us so badly; that without our help God will not be able to fulfil his promises or do his work. Surely we see in the Scriptures that God is giving men the privilege and blessing of being part of his sovereign purposes, and where some will not take that privilege he lovingly deigns to use others who will. This is illustrated well during the time of the New Testament church, as God moved the missionary sending-centre from Jerusalem to Antioch. You will recall that the Jerusalem church became authoritarian, somewhat indolent and not a little over-proud of their heritage, in a way that affected their attitude to the spread of the gospel into the Gentile world. But Christ's unconditional promise that 'he would build his church' was not thwarted because the church in Antioch was more prepared and ready to share in the joy and privilege of God's purposes.

## A vital premise

In considering the biblical basis for mission, I believe that we must begin with the all-important concept that all our considerations are based on the fact that in character and essence God, in all his ways, is complete in himself. This is why God is uniquely God, above every other being created by him. If almighty God had need of anything he would no longer be God. The writer of Ecclesiastes, which was probably Solomon, expresses it in this way:

> I know that everything God does will endure for ever; nothing can be added to it and nothing taken from it. God does it so that men will revere him
>
> (Ecclesiastes 3:14).

A. W. Tozer personalized this thought with these words:

> *I could never offer myself to a God that needed me. If He needed me, I could not respect Him, and if I could not respect Him, I could not worship Him.*[1]

Two brief Scriptures take us into profound and infinite truths that are, in reality, beyond our comprehension.

In the beginning God...

(Genesis 1:1).

In the beginning was the Word, and the Word was with God, and the Word was God

(John 1:1).

Here, as a statement of fact, without any attempt of explanation or proof, we are taken into pre-creation eternity, before the existence of the laws of time and space, where there was only God — the self-existent God, the Trinity, complete in every way, having no need of anything. But even then, although God did not need man in order to make himself complete, the picture is one of God graciously planning the forgiveness, redemption and salvation of man whom he was yet to create.

The apostle John writes of 'the Lamb that was slain from the creation of the world' (Revelation 13:8). This Lamb is slain so that fallen man can be redeemed and written into the Book of Life. The context of this verse shows clearly that 'the Lamb' is Jesus Christ. In fact, this is the one whom John has identified as 'the Word' — the *Logos* — in the first chapter of his Gospel.

In John 1:16 the Apostle goes on to show how Jesus Christ, the eternal Son, is the *only* channel through which God dispenses his gracious benefits to his creation — benefits that can never run dry; not benefits which simply come through the church or any individual believer, but first and foremost coming through the eternal Son.

From the fulness of his [that is, Jesus Christ's] grace we
have all received one blessing after another

(John 1:16).

For of his fulness we have all received, and grace upon
grace

(NASB).

Anyone who has travelled in Eastern Europe and shared fellowship with believers in their homes will be familiar with the
overwhelming hospitality which is extended to the visitor. Although this is part of the culture, it is so obviously multiplied
by their love for those of the body of Christ. Not least of all,
it shows itself at the meal table where it seems that no matter
how much one consumes, the table is no less laden with a deli-
cious variety of dishes to further tempt, and sometimes test,
the palate. I cannot count the number of times we have got up
from an Eastern European table with the words of the brother
and sister ringing in our ears, 'You have taken so little, there's
more, please eat more.'

How like the benefits of God's mercy and grace! Always sat-
isfying, yet undiminishing. The person of Jesus Christ was one
of glory, full of grace and truth. During his earthly ministry it
was not simply what he did, but who he was, and is. What Jesus
did was in many ways secondary when compared to the fulness
and perfection of his person. Speaking of the person of Christ,
Dr Martyn Lloyd-Jones expressed it in this way:

*What differentiates Christianity from all the so-called great
religions and all the philosophies of the world is simply this: that
more important than the teaching is the Teacher.*[2]

In the light of all this, what do we have to offer such a God? Nothing other than that which he has first poured into our lives — grace upon grace!

## The privilege of service

Time and again I have been drawn to the incident recorded in Acts 3. Peter and John are going to the 3.00pm prayer/sacrifice meeting held in the Jerusalem temple. At the gate sits a man lame from his birth, hoping that some of the worshippers will take pity on him as he begs for help. Although it will be costly and eventually lead to their arrest, Peter and John, as labourers together with God, cannot simply walk on past. They ask the man to look at them face to face and although the Scripture record does not tell us exactly what he saw in these disciples, their attention gave him hope. Peter and John do not have what the man wants, but they do have what he needs and with the words, 'In the name of Jesus Christ of Nazareth, walk' (v. 6), they minister the life-changing gospel to him and the man is healed in body and soul.

The Acts 3 text tells us that all this took place at the temple gate called Beautiful. This was the main entrance into the temple and Jesus would have passed through this gate as he went into the Jerusalem temple. We know that he was there on more than one occasion. John's Gospel record tells us that Jesus was in the temple during the autumn Feast of the Tabernacles (John 7:14). Again, after cleansing the temple and possibly on the Tuesday of the week leading up to the crucifixion, Jesus taught there (Matthew 22; Mark 12; Luke 20). This was the time of the Passover. Now Pentecost came seven weeks after Passover, placing the incident with Peter and John, at most, only about three or four months after Jesus had entered through this same gate into the temple.

Could it be that the lame man was at that gate as Jesus came there? We are not told in the Scripture whether or not this was so, but since the man would obviously have been a beggar for many years, it is more than possible. If that was the case, Jesus could have healed him as he had healed many before without any aid from the disciples. Rather than that, I like to think that the loving Lord and Master simply wanted to give Peter and John the privilege and joy of serving him in this way.

Whether such a view of this incident is acceptable or not, I reiterate that until we recognize that the fulfilment of the Great Commission is not motivated by what we think we can do for the living God, but by who he is and what he has purposed, our ministry will be of no eternal value.

My gracious Lord, I own Thy right
To every service I can pay;
And call it my supreme delight
To hear Thy dictates and obey.

What is my being but for Thee,
Its sure support, its noblest end;
Thy ever-smiling face to see,
And serve the cause of such a Friend?
(Philip Doddridge, 1702-51)

Paul, the missionary apostle, was more aware than most that God is not only concerned to reconcile sinful men and women to himself but also to use 'ambassadors of Christ' through which to effect this work. But in dealing with the dangerous and invasive 'I', Paul always strikes the balance when referring to his calling and ministry. For example, in writing to the Corinthians, note how carefully he chooses his words.

> But by the grace of God I am what I am, and his grace to me was not without effect. No, I worked harder than all of them — yet not I, but the grace of God that was with me
>
> (1 Corinthians 15:10).

The apostle Paul is in no doubt that it is Christ who does the work of mission. We say we believe this. Do our actions validate our words?

Are we ready to obey Christ by subjugating our personal plans and preferences to his design, whatever this might be for our lives?

Can we join with the apostle Paul in stating before God: 'I worked harder than all of them'?

# 4.
# Mission – the unfolding theme of the Old Testament

A sense of anticipation and excitement filled the classroom as a new student group gathered for the beginning of their two-year Bible study programme. Although the Republic of Moldova looked as grey and depressed as ever, the faces of the students seemed to light up the room. Eyes that had rarely seen Bible study materials in their own language gazed in disbelief as they surveyed the books carefully placed in neat piles on the tables in front of them. Under Communism the printing or importation of such literature was forbidden. Thankfully that situation had changed and these books given by Slavic Gospel Association at the beginning of the course provided a personal study library for each of the students. As they were intently examined by each student, one brother said, 'Please tell the believers in the UK who have made this possible, that these books will not sit on our shelves gathering dust — this is such a precious gift.' It seemed that he expressed what everyone was feeling, as a nod of assent went round the room.

Some of the titles needed explanation, not least of all one dealing with biblical interpretation and containing the word 'hermeneutics'. Realizing that most of the students would not have heard of this before, I was attempting to give some clarification, but the quizzical looks thrown in my direction indicated that I was only causing more confusion. Eventually, one student in his mid-forties interrupted with a question. 'Brother Trevor, why don't you just give us the chapter and verse in our Bibles where this word appears and we will understand?' Now, to meet that request was very difficult, in fact impossible, but what thrilled my heart was that here was a Moldovan brother who was *thinking biblically* as a matter of course. It was second nature to him. As we have ministered among East European Christians, one lesson we have learned repeatedly is the important mark of a true child of God — to 'think biblically'. Maybe if the Scriptures, in their various forms and translations, had not become so readily available to us in the UK, we too would be more prone to see their importance in our lives and consequently our Christian service! Certainly when considering the question of 'mission', its emphasis comes as a golden thread running through the rich tapestry of Scripture. Therefore, beginning with the Old Testament, it is important for us to spend a little time with this unfolding theme, as it runs throughout God's Word, the Bible.

## The God of Covenant

*At first sight the Old Testament appears to offer little basis for the idea of missions. This part of the Bible speaks of bloody wars and the annihilation of various heathen peoples. It appears to have very little room for mercy, nor does it seem ready to grant the blessings of the gospel to the heathen. The entire pagan world is portrayed more as a constant threat and temptation to Israel, than as an area in which God will reveal His salvation.*

So writes the Dutch missionary theologian, J. H. Bavinck,[1] and he then continues with this important comment:

*yet, if we would only investigate the Old Testament more thoroughly, it becomes clear that the future of the nations is a point of the greatest concern.*

Bavinck then continues with these helpful thoughts:

*a. The Bible repeatedly refers to the whole of mankind, as a creation of God.*

*b. This idea of creation naturally implies God's jurisdiction over the whole world. (Psalm 24: 'The earth is the LORD's, and everything in it, the world, and all who live in it.')*

*c. It is for this reason that the particular emphasis in the Old Testament of serving other gods is so strongly forbidden.*

*d. Through 'covenant' the Lord God is related to Israel in a unique act of grace that differentiates Israel from other nations and religions that only come about by law keeping, coercion and conquest.*

*e. This unmerited covenant relationship was to be lived out by Israel as a testimony to the whole world and for the benefit of the whole of mankind with the potential for Gentiles coming into this covenant relationship also.*

*f. The unifying truth is that above all, this is for the glory of Jehovah, even more than the needs of Israel or the Gentile nations.*

As God created Adam and Eve, his *covenantal* blessing and charge to them was to 'Be fruitful and increase in number; fill *the earth* and subdue it' (Genesis 1:28). The same was repeated to Noah after the destruction of the Great Flood (Genesis 6:18; 9:1).

As we saw in the previous chapter, Genesis 1:1 and John1:1 are intrinsically linked together in terms of God's worldview. Equally these verses are the basis of God's purpose as expressed in the Great Commission of Matthew 28:16-20. In direct opposition to this, John 1:11 summarizes the history of fallen mankind's response: 'He came to that which was his own, but his own did not receive him.' It is for this reason that the solemn agreement called 'covenant', made by God with man, could not be the result of a negotiation between equal partners. The Old Testament covenants could only be established as an expression of God's grace, forged in heaven before the foundation of the earth. As Bavinck goes on to suggest, this means that,

> *the work of mission is possible only within the concept of covenant*

and that,

> *(Israel's) distinction consists precisely in the fact that it may and shall be the means by which other nations shall one day receive the salvation of Israel's God.*[2]

## Mission as expressed in Eden

Genesis 3:15 stands as a great signpost that points forward to a time in history of great victory over sin and Satan. Turning from the physical to the spiritual serpent Satan, God says,

And I will put enmity between you and the woman, and between your seed and her Seed; he shall bruise your head, and you shall bruise his heel

(NKJV).

Adam and Eve have sinned and in the midst of the curses expressed in Genesis 3 as God's righteous judgement on sin verse 15 stands as a beacon of hope, being the first pronouncement of 'the gospel' — the message of mission. As the descendant of Eve, the day was foretold when Christ would defeat Satan and his 'children', and while Satan would cause Christ to suffer, he destroys Satan with a deathblow through the sacrifice of Calvary and the resurrection.

The reference here to 'the seed' is of particular importance since the whole of the book of Genesis, rather than being simply a series of unconnected stories or characters, portrays a particular divinely chosen family lineage through which God's *covenantal* pronouncement of Genesis 3:15 would be fulfilled. Through this, fallen mankind would be reconciled to God and brought back into harmonious fellowship with him. Maybe this is why the parables spoken by the Saviour telling of the 'searching shepherd', the 'seeking woman' and the 'waiting father' as recorded in Luke 15, include a glimpse into heaven, where 'the angels of God rejoice over one sinner who repents'.

Here we see 'mission accomplished' in relation to that repentant sinner, for the angels who were there at creation see something of Eden restored and God glorified. No wonder it causes them to rejoice!

## Mission as expressed through Abraham and beyond

At first glance it seems that the Genesis account of God's dealings with Abraham is recording a God of injustice as he selects individuals, families and nations as beneficiaries of his blessings, while bringing only judgement on the remainder of mankind. But a closer look at all that surrounds Abraham reveals something of God's underlying purpose in these things. His story commences in Genesis 11:27 and concludes in 25:11, the key verses being 1-3 in chapter 12.

> The LORD had said to Abram, 'Leave your country, your people and your father's household and go to the land I will show you. I will make you into a great nation and I will bless you; I will make your name great, and you will be a blessing. I will bless those who bless you, and whoever curses you I will curse; and all peoples on earth will be blessed through you.'

All that we read of Abraham relates in some way to these verses and their fulfilment. While God speaks of numerous descendants and a land, at that moment Abraham has neither, and major obstacles lie in the way of these things becoming a reality. Similarly, in contrast to men trying to 'make a name for themselves' by ignoring God's ways (Genesis 11:4), the Lord will make Abraham a man of renown. The promise that Abraham's descendants would become a great nation necessitates 'a land' in which to live, for without their own land a people could not be considered to be a nation.

Why then does God make such a covenant with Abraham? Why the promise of a great name, of being the recipient of

God's blessing and the promise of a land? The conclusion to verse 3 sounds out the clear and undeniable reason: 'and all peoples on earth will be blessed through you'. God has chosen Abraham as the channel through whom he would reach the whole of mankind with the message of salvation. The Abrahamic Covenant gives the divine plan for understanding redemptive history which culminates in 'God made flesh and dwelling among us'. Here we meet for the first time the truth that unfolds throughout the rest of the book of Genesis, namely, that through Abraham's 'seed' God's blessing will be mediated to fallen humanity. Church growth writer, Eddie Gibbs, reminds us:

> Israel was called by God to be a witnessing people. The form of her witness is not so much a missionary force as a magnetic presence. Her quality of life was intended to demonstrate to the surrounding nations that God was in her midst. As a consequence they would be attracted to Jerusalem where the throne of God was located to enjoy His presence and offer Him sacrifice and service.[3]

The apostle Paul writes in the Galatian letter with respect to this great truth:

> The Scripture foresaw that God would justify the Gentiles by faith, and announced the gospel in advance to Abraham: 'All nations will be blessed through you.' So those who have faith are blessed along with Abraham, the man of faith
>
> (Galatians 3:8-9).

Or again,

> He redeemed us in order that the blessing given to
> Abraham might come to the Gentiles through Christ
> Jesus, so that by faith we might receive the promise of
> the Spirit
>
> (Galatians 3:14).

This truth is developed further in Genesis 17 with Abram's name being changed to Abraham (v. 5) and the extended promise that 'kings of peoples' will come from Sarai, Abraham's wife (v. 16).

By changing Abram's name, God emphasizes that he will not simply be the father of a nation, but the father of many nations, not as his natural descendants but as the divine channel of blessing beyond the nation of Israel. The fact that Abraham and Sarai's descendants will include 'kings' moves us through the covenant made with Moses to that made with David and the royal line that is established, to subsequently culminate in the birth of Christ Jesus as 'great David's greater Son'. It is in this context that the psalms of David and Solomon are permeated with a worldwide missionary outlook and spirit. Typical of this is Psalm 72.

> All nations will be blessed through him, and they will call
> him blessed... Praise be to his glorious name for ever;
> may the whole earth be filled with his glory. Amen and
> Amen
>
> (vv. 17, 19).

## Mission as expressed through the prophets

The three leading roles in Old Testament Israel are that of prophet, priest and king. This in itself pointed forward to the

Lord Jesus Christ who, in his kingly and redemption work, exemplified each of these in all their perfection. However, in spite of the covenants that God had set in place, Israel proved to be a wayward and wilful people. Just as Christ is called to fulfil these offices in order to reconcile sinful man to God, so the prophets of Israel were there to call Israel to keep the covenants. In general, the Old Testament prophets were concerned with 'heralding' four major areas of truth:

1. truths concerning the character, purposes and ordinances of God;
2. truths warning and appealing to those living in sinful ways;
3. truths exhorting and comforting those who were trusting God;
4. truths relating to events that were yet to be.

Equally it is significant that the apostle Peter, in appealing to the Old Testament in his sermon in Solomon's Porch, points to the fact that the prophets were linked to the Abrahamic covenant and had their full and final fulfilment in Christ (Acts 3:22-24).

So it is that we see the prophets of Israel being raised up by God to fulfil an important and significant place in the nation's history. But again, a closer study of the prophets reveals that the richest missionary teaching given in the Old Testament comes to us through them. Most are familiar with the stories of Jonah and Daniel, the two 'missionary prophets'. These in themselves reveal again God's merciful concern poured out to others outside of the Jewish nation. But even a cursory glance at the writings of some of the other prophets underlines repeatedly God's gracious worldwide purpose.

'Here is my servant, whom I uphold, my chosen one in whom I delight; I will put my Spirit on him and *he will bring justice to the nations*'

(Isaiah 42:1).

'Turn to me and be saved, *all you ends of the earth*; for I am God, and there is no other'

(Isaiah 45:22).

'...for my house will be called a house of prayer *for all nations*'

(Isaiah 56:7).

'*For the earth* will be filled with the knowledge of the glory of the LORD, as the waters cover the sea'

(Habakkuk 2:14).

In the last days the mountain of the LORD's temple will be established... *Many nations will come and say,* 'Come, let us go up to the mountain of the LORD'

(Micah 4:1-2).

'*And many peoples and powerful nations* will come to Jerusalem to seek the LORD Almighty and to entreat him'

(Zechariah 8:22).

These are but a few of the many passages from the prophetic writings, which remind us that God directs his purposes not to one select group, people or type, but to the whole earth.

The continual challenge to the nation of Israel was to be open to the truth that God was making a way for other nations to respond to his Word and his ways. The temple contained a special court for the Gentiles but there is little evidence in the Old Testament of a welcoming spirit being extended to those who would come there. In fact, all too often Israel was anything but the testimony that God intended it to be. In contrast to the New Testament church, the witness in the Old Testament was to be not so much by 'going', but rather by 'being' that which God had purposed his people to be.

The prophet Jeremiah expresses it in this way:

'If you will return, O Israel, return to me,' declares the LORD. '…and if in a truthful, just and righteous way you swear, "As surely as the LORD lives," then the nations will be blessed by him and in him they will glory'

(Jeremiah 4:1-2).

By being what God intended his people to be and by obediently going where he directs, we have that which lies at the heart of mission.

In this chapter we have come full circle from Eden to Malachi and back to the promise of Genesis 3:15. It appears that the Israel of the Old Testament so often missed the sense of wonder and privilege which God had afforded to them, as the instrument of his message of mercy and grace to a lost world. As the church of Christ today, maybe we should address this question: How can we learn from the errors of the Old Testament people of God and seek to fulfil the purposes of God for his people today, in taking the good news to the whole world?

# 5.
# From the heart of God

Imagine that forty different men were selected over sixteen centuries, from varied cultures and callings of life, to contribute a chapter each for a book on theology. Could there be any expectation that one unified book would result? Surely the answer must be a resounding 'no', since producing a book using this approach could only work against its unity. Yet the Bible, which came into being in this way, can clearly be seen to be *one Book* and, above all, this attests to its divine authorship. As A. W. Pink points out:

> ...behind the many parts of the Bible is an unmistakable organic unity as shown in its one system of doctrine, one code of ethics, one plan of salvation and one rule of faith.[1]

The more one studies the Bible in an open-minded manner, the more one is convinced that behind its human authorships is an overruling and directing 'mastermind'. One proof of this is the manner in which a whole range of themes is found to run throughout both Old and New Testaments, one striking illustration being the theme of 'mission'. Having briefly traced this through the Old Testament Scriptures, it is helpful to see how it will inevitably continue in the New Testament. This must be so, since 'mission' is so dear to the heart of God.

The inter-testamental period lasted for approximately four hundred years. As the prophets became silent no other inspired writer was raised up. During this period the Persian Empire fell to the power of Greece, which in turn was overrun by the rise of the Roman Empire.

Other extra-biblical writers of this period recorded it to be a time of great affliction for the nation of Israel. Yet God was preparing the world to receive its Redeemer and Saviour.

But when the time had fully come, God sent his Son, born of a woman, born under law, to redeem those under law, that we might receive the full rights of sons
(Galatians 4:4).

## The place of the Great Commission in Matthew's Gospel

It is little wonder that in establishing the New Testament canon, the early Church Fathers placed Matthew's Gospel at the beginning. He was a Jew among Jews and, as such, looked for the Messiah-King long promised in the Law and the Prophets of the Old Testament Scriptures. Matthew's Gospel writings, therefore, give the perfect bridge from Old to New Testament, concluding with Matthew 28:16-20 — the Great Commission — as the focal point of his Gospel.

These last verses are no mere thoughts to neatly round off the presentation of Jesus as the Messiah but, rather, have been building up, like an orchestral symphony, to culminate in the resounding finale of exemplified power and mandate of Jesus Christ, the King of Kings. From the beginning of Matthew chapter one there are several signposts which move us to draw this conclusion.

## The sequence of Matthew 1:1

> A record of the genealogy of Jesus Christ the son of David, the son of Abraham
>
> ( Matthew 1:1).

In verse one, under the inspiration of the Holy Spirit, Matthew sets the sequence from David back to Abraham, then reverses this order from verse two and, beginning with Abraham, traces the genealogy through David, the father of Solomon (v. 6) to 'Jesus, who is called Christ' (v. 16). In Jewish thought the latter would have been the obvious and accepted pattern by which to express our Lord's genealogy. Gibbs comments:

> *...through succeeding centuries Abraham presents a constant challenge to the people of God. He confronts their complacency and serves as a reminder of the saving initiative of God. Our Lord challenged those who presumed to say 'We have Abraham as our Father,' by telling them that God was able to make descendants for Abraham even from the stones scattered around them (Matt. 3:9).*[2]

From the sequence of Matthew 1:1 we can only conclude that something of vital importance is being stated which supersedes the genealogy order that follows. Clearly, in referring to Christ as the son or *seed* of David, Matthew is establishing his sovereign kingship above all else. The Old Testament emphasizes that the 'throne of David' was more than an 'earthly' throne. This is clearly shown as David's son Solomon succeeds to that throne.

> So Solomon sat on *the throne of the LORD* as king in place of his father David...
>
> (1 Chronicles 29:23).

It is from the 'throne of the Lord' that Christ can rightly claim 'All authority in heaven and on earth has been given to me' (Matthew 28:18). Matthew establishes this truth from the first sentence of his Gospel. Then, as the *seed* of Abraham, Matthew portrays the human nature of Christ linked back through Abraham to the covenant of Genesis 3:15 previously referred to. This is underlined further in Matthew 1:2 in that 'Abraham was the father of Isaac…' In this we recall that Isaac was born miraculously 'through promise' as God brought together the supernatural and the natural in order to maintain that 'seed-*line*'.

## The genealogy of Matthew 1 and beyond

Against all the prejudice, tradition and custom of Judaism, women appear in Matthew's genealogy of Christ. Even more amazingly some of these are Gentiles.

Salmon the father of Boaz, whose mother was Rahab,
Boaz the father of Obed, whose mother was Ruth
(Matthew 1:5).

Here is a startling reminder that Jesus Christ is to be the Saviour of the world and not only of the Jews. This finds Matthew already echoing the mandate of Matthew 28:19 to 'go to all nations'. In choosing to name Rahab, Matthew draws our attention to a notorious sinner and foreigner well known to those familiar with Old Testament Scripture. Equally Ruth is a foreigner received into the nation of Israel. Both of these examples cause us to think again of the immensity of God's grace extended to Jew and Gentile alike. Within a few more sentences this Jewish writer, Matthew, is recording the visit to Jerusalem of wise men from 'the East' seeking to worship the infant Christ.

This worldview continues throughout the Gospel, when the healing of a centurion's servant brings this retort from Jesus, 'King of the Jews', 'I tell you the truth, I have not found anyone in Israel with such great faith,' (8:10). By chapter 15 we are reading of a woman of Canaan pleading with Jesus to meet the need of her demon-possessed daughter and Jesus, commending her faith, answers her prayers. Chapter 25 speaks of the time when 'the Son of Man comes in his glory', when 'all the nations will be gathered before him, and he will separate the people one from another...' (vv. 31-32). This separation is not by race but between believers and unbelievers.

Finally, at the cross of Christ, Matthew records a centurion declaring, 'Surely he was the Son of God!' (27:54). It is most unlikely that this man was of the Jewish nation. Although an earthquake and the opening of tombs accompanied the death of Christ, the centurion saw beyond all this and unlike many of the Jews, with a heart that had not been hardened, he makes this valued judgement of the Saviour. Legend has it that he became a Christian. Even if that was not so the great reminder is that both the Jewish and the Gentile world was embraced at Calvary.

## Matthew 28:16-20

Considering Matthew 28:16-20 in some detail, observe how these verses unfold.

## a. *Obedience and the King (v. 16)*

Why should eleven disillusioned followers of Christ gather on an unnamed mountainside in an area of Galilee in northern Palestine? Why should they have trekked about 100 miles from Jerusalem where all their hopes and aspirations had come crashing to the ground? There were reports that their crucified Master was risen, but they were yet to see that for themselves! Beyond all reason, it seems that they gathered on that mountainside simply because Jesus had told them to do so.

> Then the eleven disciples went to Galilee, to the mountain where Jesus had told them to go
>
> (v. 16).

Their surrender to the word of Christ was greater than their fears and discouragements, despite the fact that 'some doubted'. First and foremost the Great Commission is founded on obedience to the Word of God. It is for this reason that the mode and method of true mission can never contravene the Scriptures.

## b. *Worship and the King (v. 17)*

> When they saw him, they worshipped him.

The appearance of the risen Lord caused them to worship him. It has been said that a worshipping people will inevitably be a witnessing people because true worship is a lifestyle. Throughout the New Testament the thought of 'worship' and 'service' is continually interchanged in translating the original text. I would suggest that the Great Commission only becomes relevant through worship. As Warren Wiersbe comments:

*When the church gathers to worship, it also gathers to witness. That witness is threefold: to the Lord, to the church itself and to the world… Of these three, the most important is our witness to the Lord for if that is amiss we will not be able to edify one another or evangelize the lost.*[3]

Therefore we see that the context of the Great Commission is not one of a world in need or even the expansion of the church, but of obedience to the Word of God that leads the disciple to worship the living God.

### c. *Authority and the King* (v. 18)

Thankfully the Great Commission is not programme driven but empowered through Christ's authority.

Then Jesus came to them and said, 'All authority in heaven and on earth has been given to me.'

Jesus makes this all-embracing claim to authority. He did not seize it, for it had been given to him as his right by the Godhead. There is neither place, nor time, nor even heaven nor eternity that falls outside the Lord's sovereign authority. These were similar phrases of prayer to those he taught the disciples (Matthew 6). Now Jesus asserts these truths again in order that those he is commissioning in mission might be assured that they go with his power. As his subjects, he delegates to his disciples the right and the responsibility to carry the message of the Kingdom to the nations and this message is one that demands full allegiance, for to be his follower, each must own his right to rule over them as their sovereign Lord.

### d. *The subjects and their King* (v. 19)

'Therefore go and make disciples of all nations.'

In this verse the stress is not upon the 'going' but rather on the 'making of disciples'. The key word is 'therefore'. By inference Jesus is saying that because they have obeyed his word, because they truly worship him and because all authority is his, delegated to them as his disciples ... of course they will go. He does not have to command them to go, their burning desire will be to go. In this way the 'going' becomes a matter of consequence found in the disciple's heart, rather than a command to be coldly obeyed. Mission then becomes a matter of the disciple catching the heartbeat of the Master.

The 'making of disciples' will not only involve 'going', but will also be fulfilled through 'teaching' and 'baptizing'; but of even more importance, we recall that it is Christ who is uttering these words, the one who 'made disciples' as no other. It is one thing to teach discipleship, and this is probably more essential today than ever before, but the command is to 'make disciples'. In this there is no quick fix or short circuit. It is a costly business. It cost God his only begotten Son and as Christ came he made disciples by engaging life-to-life, person-to-person. The Gospels record how he dined and prayed, encouraged and rebuked and even wept with his disciples as he taught them the profound spiritual truths of the kingdom. The implication for each of us is that only those who are disciples themselves can be used of the Lord to make disciples.

One of the most humbling occasions we can recall came our way some three years after the sweeping revolutions that brought about the fall of Communism across Europe. We were meeting with a group of Eastern European pastors to discuss future plans, when one brother said, 'Before we get down to the details of the day can I say on behalf of all the brothers here how we have appreciated the ministry of Slavic Gospel Association. For us the important thing is that the S.G.A. missionaries came to share fellowship with us in the days when we were really hurting under the heel of Communism. This will always be very precious to us.'

In relation to the book *Glimpses of God's Grace*, Dr Paul Negrut, President of Emanuel Christian University, Oradea, Romania, and President of the Baptist Union of Romania wrote:

> *In spite of all the restrictions imposed by the past Communist regime of Romania, S.G.A. had the vision and courage to come and suffer with us, work alongside us, pray for us and invest in us. Words are insufficient to describe the calibre of the work and impact S.G.A. has had in Romania over the last 35 years.*[4]

Although no foreign mission can ever claim perfection in its ministry, undoubtedly we live in days when national Christians are looking for this kind of understanding and commitment from foreign missionaries. Without question, the long-term 'partnership' approach followed by a number of mission agencies has enhanced the effectiveness of their ministries in Eastern Europe, particularly since the onset of the fall of Communism.

But to return to the Great Commission in Matthew 28, notice our final reference.

### e.  *A promise by the King* (v. 20)

'And surely I am with you always, to the very end of the age.'

This will be considered in more detail later, but for the moment we simply need to note that the disciple goes with *all* authority, to *all* nations, to teach *all* things that he has commanded knowing that he is with us *always*.

Go forth and tell! O Church of God, awake!
God's saving news to all the nations take:
Proclaim Christ Jesus, Saviour, Lord and King,
That all the world His worthy praise may sing.

(J. E. Seddon, 1915-83)


## The place of the Great Commission in John's Gospel

Similar lines of study could be conducted through the Gospels of Mark and Luke, but in many ways Matthew's Gospel is typical of the theme of mission as it flows through the synoptic Gospels. However, before moving on, it is beneficial to pause in the Gospel of John in order to consider 'the heartbeat of God' further. Unlike the other Gospel writers John gives us his clear purpose statement in penning this Gospel, a statement that could be adopted by any local church or mission agency when considering the reason for engaging in mission.

'…but these [things] are written that you may believe that Jesus is the Christ, the Son of God, and that by believing you may have life in his name'

(John 20:31).

But turning from the end of John's Gospel to its beginning, John 1:1 immediately confronts us with another major difference when compared to the beginning of the Gospels of Matthew, Mark and Luke.

> In the beginning was the Word, and the Word was with God, and the Word was God. He was with God in the beginning
>
> (John 1:1).

Whereas the synoptic Gospels begin at the time Jesus came to earth and give his human genealogy, John's Gospel begins in eternity when Christ the Word was 'face to face' with God the Father prior to any creative act. This reminds us again of the link back to Genesis 1:1 ('In the beginning God created the heavens and the earth') as previously mentioned in chapter 3 of this book.

John is so taken with the astounding truth of Jesus as 'God made flesh dwelling among us' that time and again he returns to the theme of the mission that Jesus is fulfilling on behalf of the Godhead. It is reckoned that there are forty-six occasions where John's Gospel tells us of the Father sending his Son, or of Christ as the Sent One. For example, Jesus prays,

> '[Father,] as you sent me into the world, I have sent them into the world'
>
> ( 17:18).

Or again,

> ...Jesus said, '...As the Father has sent me, I am sending you'
>
> (20:21).

Equally, John 14:26 speaks of the involvement of the Father
and the Son in sending the Holy Spirit:

> 'But the Counsellor, the Holy Spirit, whom the Father
> will send in my name, will teach you all things...'

This leads us further into the continuing theme of mission as it
unfolds in the New Testament, where the word 'apostle' from
the Greek word *'apostello'* ('I send') is a synonym for the word
'missionary' from the Latin *'mitto'* ('I send').

So often we think of the apostle Paul as the model missionary,
but here John is drawing us to gaze on one far, far greater than
Paul, even our Saviour, the Great Apostle, the 'missionary' par
excellence.

William Hendriksen's comment on John 17:18 is helpful
here. He writes:

> *Jesus is still thinking of 'The Word', the message of redemption*
> *in Christ to the glory of God. It is in this connection He makes*
> *a double comparison; that is, between the Father as Sender and*
> *Himself as Sender, and between Himself as Sent and the disciples*
> *as having been sent. The two comparisons blend into one idea,*
> *which is this, just as the Father has sent Jesus into the world with*
> *a message, so also Jesus has sent the disciples into the world with*
> *a message. The message, moreover, is the same, that of redemption*
> *in Christ.*[5]

In realizing that we are all sinners by nature and so easily
deceived, we need to be constantly lifting our eyes from
comparing ourselves, or 'our' church, with others and with what
they may or may not be doing. If this is the measure by which
we judge our concern for mission, we will have no problem

in justifying and even commending ourselves. The true plumb line is our God in the person of Jesus Christ.

> Therefore, holy brothers, who share in the heavenly calling, fix your thoughts on Jesus, the apostle and high priest whom we confess. He was faithful to the one who appointed him…
>
> (Hebrews 3:1-2).

Such words of Scripture ought to cause us to consider continually just how much of our concept and understanding of 'mission' is Christ-centred! As pastors and preachers, is he at the heart of our teaching on mission?

As we all seek to engage in mission activity, is Christ truly the object of our service and ministry?

# 6.
# Through the heart of the church

The spring of 1990 found us in Prague's Old Town Square again, admiring the Jan Hus monument. Since our last visit the so-called 'Velvet Revolution' had taken place in Czechoslovakia, bringing with it the downfall of the Communist control of the country. In contrast to these 'bloodless' events of a few months earlier, our minds were cast back not only to 6 July 1415 when Jan Hus was burned at the stake for his faith in the city of Constanz, but also to how Hus's preaching and writings encouraged new editions of the Czech Bible and a flourishing increase in the production of Christian Czech literature. So much so, that in the mid-1400s the Roman Catholic Cardinal Piccolomini, later to become Pope Pius II, was led to the amazing realization that 'many a Hussite peasant woman knew the Bible better than many Roman priests and men of high ecclesiastical rank'.

In the Czech lands of Bohemia and Moravia, Christianity dates back to the end of the eighth century. Early in the tenth century the famous Prince Vaclav, better known as 'Good King Wenceslas', became an important propagator of a profound and peaceable Christian piety which, although sincere, eventually called for the refining fires of the Czech Reformation of the fifteenth century to cause the Czech church to burn with the evangelical fervour of mission.

Towards the close of the fourteenth century Richard II of England married Anne of Bohemia, the daughter of Czech King Vaclav IV. This in turn led to Czech students studying in Oxford, from where they brought the teaching of English reformer John Wyclif to Prague.

*One such was Jerome of Prague. He returned to his own city full of zeal for the truths he had learned in England, and taught boldly that the Roman Church had fallen away from the doctrine of Christ and that everyone who sought salvation must come back to the teachings of the Gospel. Among many on whose hearts such words fell with power was Jan Hus.*[1]

God used Wyclif's influence as the last impulse needed to fan the flames of the Czech Reformation into life under Hus's leadership. In a letter addressed to a colleague of John Wyclif and dated September 1410, Jan Hus wrote:

*I must tell you dear brother, that the people will listen to nothing but the holy Scriptures, especially the Gospels and the Epistles. Wherever in city or town, in village or castle, the preacher of the holy truth makes his appearance, the people flock together in crowds, despising the clergy of the Church who are unable to bring such teaching.*

It was a short walk from the Old Town Square to '*Vaclavske Namesti*', Wenceslas Square, and with an hour to spare before moving on, we joined the bustling crowds near the statue which heads the long thoroughfare leading to the square. Unlike the times we had known under Communism, there seemed to be a spring in everyone's step and an expectant yet relaxed atmosphere filled the air. Two sizable crowds could be seen on opposite sides of the square. They were gathered around long tables set out on the respective pavements and laden with Czech literature. To our amazement one table was manned by two followers of Hare Krishna, evident by their shaven heads, saffron-coloured robes and two perpendicular marks on their foreheads, signifying slavery to Lord Krishna. We discovered later that the second table carried literature published by the Jehovah's Witness organization. These were 'heady' days and with great enthusiasm and excitement the people were devouring the attractively produced books and pamphlets as if there was no tomorrow.

Two days later in the welcoming home of a Czech pastor we had come to know over the preceding years, we talked of what we had witnessed in Prague. Pastor Pavel shook his head slowly from side to side and said in a sombre tone of voice, 'We were simply not ready. With all of our history as the church of Jesus Christ and of preaching the gospel, we were simply not ready.'

My heart went out to Pavel. How could they have been ready for such dramatic changes with all the restrictions that the Communist regime had placed upon the church? Surely the real question was why we, as Western believers, had not been more thoughtful and concerned to help them be ready; particularly as it was obvious that the Hare Krishna and Jehovah's Witness movements had given attention to this, at least as far as their preparation of literature in the Czech language was concerned.

However, it is true that, in general terms, the church in Eastern Europe developed a 'siege mentality' under Communism, especially in some of the harsher situations. In many instances, particularly among an older generation of leaders, the philosophy appeared to be one of 'let's pull up the drawbridge and be prepared to die for what we have'; and who can point a critical finger at our brothers and sisters for this! We ought never to forget that many were called upon to pay that ultimate price.

Even so, many in leadership in the churches faced great difficulty in making the challenging transition from 'defence to attack' in the context of the new openness and freedoms which came with the fall of Communism. New opportunities had to be taken on board in the realization that the fundamental biblical principle is that God seeks to reach 'the world' through his church and in particular, his 'local church'. David Jackman makes the following pertinent observation:

> It is largely the health of the local churches that determines the progress of the work of God in any locality or nation.[2]

Having considered 'a siege mentality' in Eastern Europe, the question is whether things are different elsewhere in the world. Secularism, materialism and apathy bring their own challenge to the relevance of today's church and the message of the gospel. In reality, have our local churches been any more prepared than many of the churches in Eastern Europe when great changes have confronted them? Do we really believe that God's order is 'from his heart', through the heart of the church, to the heart of the world? Are we seriously addressing such questions as why the church of Jesus Christ exists? Are we fulfilling the reason for which the Lord has left his church here in the world, or are we simply becoming more and more absorbed by the modern methods and techniques of local church activities? It is said that a fanatic can be defined as 'a person who redoubles his efforts when he has forgotten his aim'. Such a comment may bring a smile, but with all the possibilities and 'tools' that are now available to us, are we not guilty all too often of becoming addicted to the 'how' rather than the 'why' of local church life?

## Metaphorically speaking

One does not have to look too deeply into today's Western society to recognize that, more than ever, man is feeling a deep-seated need to belong to a 'community'. In speaking with Eastern European Christians through the days of Communism, isolation was one of the powerful weapons used by the secret police against the believers, as they attempted to break their spirit. In some cases this meant solitary confinement in a prison cell, for others it was an extended period of internal exile to some remote area away from family and familiar surroundings. It is good to pause from time to time to read the experience of those who have suffered such things first hand. The biography of close friend and brother in the gospel, Bulgarian pastor, Hristo Kulichev,[3] imprisoned as late as 1985, is well worth such a read. Of this Dr John Killenger[4] writes:

> *Christians have enjoyed a remarkable tradition of prison literature, from St Paul to John Bunyan to Dietrich Bonhoeffer. Now we can add to that tradition the story of Bulgarian pastor Hristo Kulichev, whose stalwart faith during years of Communist harassment and imprisonment has already become legendary. His ringing declaration, 'I prefer to be in prison with Jesus than to be free without Him,' will reverberate in our hearts forever, inspiring new faithfulness in every generation.*

In the UK we see that sense of community through family ties and relationships, of which Hristo Kulichev was deprived for the gospel's sake, becoming eroded and under increasing threat through an array of other reasons. Consequently this leads to the need to belong, which is exemplified in a multitude of other ways. Many find their fulfilment in joining others in the worship of sport, or through association with such societies as the Freemasons or some 'good cause'. Young professionals increasingly gravitate to the clubs and wine bars, which now provide what others find at the public house. For some, the bingo hall provides the one weekly possibility of feeling part of a 'family'. The danger is that the church simply takes on the role of an alternative community, as it becomes increasingly sophisticated in providing the kind of ethos that can so readily satisfy this felt need of community.

Of course the church, both local and universal, ought to be a community, but the Bible clearly teaches that the church is unique in that it is not man-made but God-created, organically related to Christ and dependent on him for its existence, life and message. The reality is that it is all too possible to lead someone into a Christian lifestyle without them knowing God in terms of a personal relationship that comes from biblical thinking and produces righteous living — surely the mark of the true Christian. The importance of this life-changing relationship is well illustrated in the seven powerful metaphors used in the Scriptures as they present the church's profile. As God looks at his church, what should he see? As the church views itself and is viewed by the world, what should be evident?

## 1. *The church as a bride in a relationship of love with the Bridegroom — Christ Jesus*

The LORD did not set his affection on you and choose you because you were more numerous than other peoples, for you were the fewest of all peoples. But it was because the LORD loved you and kept the oath he swore to your forefathers...

(Deuteronomy 7:7-8).

*Other related passages:* Ephesians 5:25-27, 31-32; Revelation 21:2; 19:7-9.

## 2. *The church as the body, belonging to each other because of being related to the Head — Christ Jesus*

> ...speaking the truth in love, we will in all things grow up into him who is the Head, that is, Christ. From him the whole body, joined and held together by every supporting ligament, grows and builds itself up in love, as each part does its work
>
> (Ephesians 4:15-16).

*Other related passages:* 1 Corinthians 12; Ephesians 1:22-23.

## 3. *The church as the flock, under Christ's shepherd care*

> 'I am the good shepherd; I know my sheep and my sheep know me — just as the Father knows me and I know the Father — and I lay down my life for the sheep'
>
> (John 10:14-15).

*Other related passages:* John 10:1-18; 1 Peter 5:2-4; Acts 20:28.

## 4. *The church as fruit-bearing branches of the vine — Christ Jesus*

> 'I am the vine, you are the branches. If a man remains in me and I in him, he will bear much fruit'
>
> (John 15:5).

*Other related passages:* John 15:1-9; John 17:22-23.

## 5. *The church as a household with Christ as the Head of the family*

For through him [Christ Jesus] we both have access to
the Father by one Spirit. Consequently, you are no longer
foreigners and aliens, but fellow-citizens with God's
people and members of God's household

(Ephesians 2:18-19).

*Other related passages*: Galatians 6:10; Genesis 12:1-3.

## 6. *The church as the temple of God — holy through Christ's righteousness*

Don't you know that you yourselves are God's temple
and that God's Spirit lives in you? ...you are that temple
(1 Corinthians 3:16-17).

*Other related passages:* Ephesians 2:19-22; 1 Peter 2:5.

## 7. *The church as a priesthood — separated unto Christ through a lifestyle of worship*

But you are a chosen people, a royal priesthood, a holy
nation, a people belonging to God, that you may declare
the praises of him who called you out of darkness into
his wonderful light

(1 Peter 2:9).

*Other related passage:* 2 Corinthians 3:18.

In this last metaphor we find an important key to understanding
why the church should exist; namely,

*that you may set forth* the wonderful deeds and display the virtues and perfections of Him Who called you out of darkness into His marvellous light

(Amplified New Testament).

## The heart of the matter

The local church is a microcosm of the universal church and, as such, two biblical concepts dominate in terms of gathering together the profile given through the seven metaphors previously mentioned. First, as we have seen from Matthew 28:17 and illustrated through the metaphors, there is the picture of the people of God as a 'worshipping people'. If void of this, the church drifts into becoming simply another form of 'community'. The second concept is the task of 'proclamation' as a witnessing people, without which the reason for the church's existence becomes meaningless and it might just as well portray itself as another club, society or community that would be good to join for the benefit of its members.

Consider for a moment the form and function of the New Testament church as expressed in the first few chapters of the Acts of the Apostles, following the powerful apostolic preaching and witness. Several emphases are clearly evident, like satellites in space orbiting a central planet, where each satellite maintains its motion and life because of its relationship to the gravitational pull of the central planet. For the New Testament church the gravitational pull upon its heart was that of 'declaring the praises of him who called you out of darkness into his wonderful light'. In other words, each form and function could only have life and meaning as it revolved around the concept of 'proclamation'. In the church of the

New Testament, the satellites of worship, leadership and discipline, teaching and preaching, sharing and giving, and even the sacraments of the Lord's Supper and baptism, only had life, meaning and direction as they revolved around the central 'planet' of proclaiming Christ in all his fulness. The grand obsession of the New Testament believers was sharing and spreading their mutual love of Christ as their Redeemer, Saviour and Lord. Everything was subordinate to this cause and we read again and again of what God did through a church so engrossed and dominated by this passion of 'missioning' Christ into the world. Two examples indicate how this was worked out in practice in the New Testament church.

In Acts 6 when the neglect of the Hellenist Jewish widows presented a potential problem that might divert the apostles from proclaiming the Word of God, the '*diakonia*' was established, as others were appointed to serve at the tables. Here is a classic example of 'organization' becoming the servant of 'proclamation'.

> So the Word of God spread. The number of disciples in Jerusalem increased rapidly...
>
> > (Acts 6:7).

The danger is that all too often we reverse this priority. Also, notice the teaching that the apostle Paul gives to the Corinthian church as he institutes the Lord's Supper.

> For whenever you eat this bread and drink this cup, you proclaim [or announce] the Lord's death until he comes
> > (1 Corinthians 11:26).

Each time the church gathers around the Lord's Table she proclaims that she believes that the message she has for the world is encapsulated in the truth of Christ crucified, risen and returning.

## Four thoughts, one aim!

The 'announcing' or 'gospel preaching' of the church is basically expressed in four ways in the New Testament. It does this by using different forms of words and concepts.

### 1. *To evangelize*

When the angel appeared to the shepherds at the time of Christ's birth we read that the angel said,

> 'I bring you good news of great joy that will be for all the people'
>
> (Luke 2:10).

Literally translated, this reads 'I *evangelize* to you great joy' and the word *'evangelizomai'* is introduced into the vocabulary. Timothy is urged by the apostle Paul to 'do the work of an evangelist' (2 Timothy 4:5). In the Ephesian letter Paul teaches that in the unity of the body of Christ (the church) and in the economy of God, 'It was he [Christ] who gave some to be ... evangelists...' (Ephesians 4:11).

### 2. *To talk the gospel*

A further extension of the *'evangelizomai'* concept is carried in Acts 8:4 where Dr Luke records that as persecution came to the Jerusalem Christians they were scattered throughout the region, but undeterred they literally 'announced the glad tidings *wherever they went'.* The inference appears to be that in the market place, over the fence, in their family and among their friends they 'talked' the gospel.

### 3. *To herald*

In the synagogue in Nazareth our Lord reads from the prophet Isaiah stating that

> 'The Spirit of the Lord is on me, because he has anointed me to preach good news to the poor. He has sent me to proclaim freedom for the prisoners … to proclaim the year of the Lord's favour'
>
> (Luke 4:18-19).

The word used here is *'kerusso'*, meaning to blaze out as a herald the good news. Referring again to the apostle Paul, he uses this same thought in stating his calling. 'And of this gospel I was appointed a herald…' (2 Timothy 1:11). The emphasis here is 'telling it as it is' as a herald would do; not what we think we ought to say or what we feel people would like to hear, but the truth as it is.

### 4. *To be a witness*

As the risen Christ appeared to the apostles he commissioned them with these words: '…and you will be my witnesses…' (Acts 1:8).

This was both a clear command and a prediction given by the Saviour. It indicated both what the church ought to do, and what it would be enabled to do. For this reason these words of Acts 1:8 are coupled with the promise of the Holy Spirit through whom this would be possible.

The 'root' meaning from which the writer of Acts drew the word witness is *'martus'*, from which the English word 'martyr' is derived. This appears no less than twelve times in the book of Acts. The thought of a martyr as one who is subject to suffering or, in an extreme case, put to death for one's belief, became a living reality to many in the New Testament church, and a normal consequence of 'proclaiming' the gospel of Jesus Christ — one that the church has come to experience throughout history!

## A living example

I have known only one person whose whole life exemplified what it means to preach Christ in all of these four ways. His name was Simon. When we first met he was already in his latter years. As an elderly retired Romanian pastor, he had lived out the whole of his ministry under a Communist dictatorship that sought to give an impression of religious tolerance to the Western world, whilst at the same time seeking to brutally crush the Christian witness. Simon had been the pastor of a registered Baptist church and although severe restrictions were placed upon its activities, at least it could gather legally within its building. Not desiring to consciously break the law, Simon simply heralded out the truths of the gospel from his pulpit week by week. His powerful and God-anointed ministry was used to draw many to personal faith in a living Lord and Saviour. In doing this his evangelistic proclamation of the gospel attracted the attention of the authorities, particularly as a growing number of young people were attending his church. Finally it all became too much for the authorities and Simon was warned to tone down his preaching and actively discourage the younger generation from coming to the meetings or 'he would suffer the consequences'. Inevitably Simon refused, making the point that, as he was not asking the Securitate to do his work of preaching, they ought not to think of asking him to do their policing. The final outcome was that his licence was withdrawn, with the consequence that he could no longer legally function as a Christian pastor and he was imprisoned on the charge of subversion.

During those long years of imprisonment his loving wife and two teenage children frequently suffered tortuous months of not knowing whether Simon was dead or alive; but throughout those years God kept him faithful even though there were many deprivations to endure for his precious Lord and Master. Upon his release the controls closed in on him and the family even further when, in a country where to be unemployed would put you in prison, he was told by the secret police that the only work he would be allowed to do was that for which they gave their permission. In an attempt to humiliate him in the town where he was still known as a pastor, they assigned to him the work of district pest exterminator, in effect, the local rat catcher.

In his quaint and attractive use of the English language Simon often said to us, 'My dears, we must remember that the ways of God not often can be discovered.' His testimony clearly declared that originally he was the pastor of a local church, but in its place the Lord gave him a large and extensive parish.

His dark eyes sparkled with joy and enthusiasm as he recounted how in the course of his work in outlying farms, factories and blocks of flats he met so many with whom he could share the gospel. 'In fact,' he said, 'in a number of places I found isolated believers who were scattered around the district and I could do my work during the day and be their pastor in the evenings.'

Simon certainly knew how to evangelize, herald, talk and witness to the gospel; and a needy world was being reached. These opportunities to spread the good news did not have to be 'manufactured' by Simon; as is always the case, they came as the natural outflow of a humble man or woman of God walking in the ways of God.

# 7.
# Into the heart of the world

Probably the greatest challenge to the church today is how to bring the unchanging good news of new life in Jesus Christ to a world that has not only seen dramatic and accelerating change in recent decades, but continues in its restless and often catastrophic quest for happiness. Most evangelical believers would agree with David Jackman, who stated:

> We must remember that the Church's mission is not to influence, or to impress, but to see all nations discipled. This is Christ's concern – to call out a universal family of God's children from every kindred and tongue, those whom He has made His disciples.[1]

The question is, do we believe that God's purpose is that the church of Jesus Christ is the channel through which this will be accomplished and that it is still possible to reach this goal? If so, then how best will this be accomplished?

## One short step for man…???

As 'the Enlightenment' of the seventeenth and eighteenth centuries shaped the thinking of Western nations, people began to believe that science and human reason would solve all the world's problems and, in doing so, meet man's deepest needs. True knowledge was seen to be inherently good, as it dealt with life's realities in terms of 'facts'. Progressive technology and scientific discovery, along with economic advancement, would eventually lead mankind to a better world, bringing with it personal happiness.

For many people in the 'modern era' science became the new religion as a source of absolute truth. Of course, such advances have brought untold benefits, but it was eventually realized that although we could put a man on the moon, nations still warred with each other, some parts of the world continued to suffer appalling famine and starvation, and many great discoveries were potentially providing a self-destruct button. The arrogance of modernity in implying that it could provide all the answers to every question was quickly becoming suspect and post-modernity began to take root. Thomas Oden maintains:

> ...the modern age lasted exactly 200 years – from the fall of the Bastille in 1789 to the fall of the Berlin Wall in 1989.[2]

In 1989 theologian Diogenes Allen affirmed that,

> ...the principles forged during the period of 'Enlightenment' which formed the foundations of modern mentality are crumbling.[3]

Inevitably post-modern thinking reacted against all that modernity had offered. In reality some of the then accepted principles, such as reasoned argument and absolute truths, provided a platform for the gospel. As modernity collapsed, so too did these tenets. Graham Johnston summarizes the change to post-modern thinking in this way.[4]

> *In the end ten distinctives emerged as the hallmark of post-modern people:*
> 1. *They are reacting to modernity and all its tenets*
> 2. *They reject objective truth*
>    *[\*that is, absolute truth]*
> 3. *They are sceptical and suspicious of authority*
> 4. *They are like missing persons in search of a self and an identity*
> 5. *They have blurred morality and are into whatever is expedient*
>    *[\*whatever 'feels' good is good]*
> 6. *They continue to search for the transcendent*
> 7. *They are living in a media world unlike any other*
>    *[\* where fiction is portrayed as fact and fact is interchanged with fiction]*
> 8. *They engage in the 'knowing smirk'*
> 9. *They are on a quest for community*
> 10. *They live in a very material world.*

(\* The author's added comments.)

With much foresight G. K. Chesterton warned, when people cease believing in God, it's not that they believe in nothing, but that they will believe in anything. Any twenty-first-century Christian concerned for lost humanity will find a familiar ring to Johnston's summary and it is important to be reminded that this is the world in which God has placed us. Another way to consider what has occurred is to note the following comparisons:[5]

| Modernity | Post-modernity |
|---|---|
| Creation | Deconstruction |
| Design | Chance |
| Purpose | Play |
| Hierarchy | Anarchy |
| A completed work | A process |
| Depth | Surface |
| Metaphysical | Irony |

We are continually reminded that we are all part of a global village that functions as never before. In consequence it reaps the inevitable results.

> *Without the external standards of truth and morality and without the internal standards brought about by a sense of self and dignity, there can only be cynicism, panic and free fall.*[6]

One tragic yet evident consequence resulting from post-modern man's thinking is that he can only function on the basis of short-term commitment. Middleton and Walsh make the following comment:

> *Indeed, instead of long-term commitment, the post-modern self just moves onto the next game, to the next show, to the next relationship.*[7]

In the previous chapters we have seen that the Great Commission is effectively God's worldview, one important consequence being that there is the potential for individuals to find eternal benefit dependent upon the acceptance of the absolute truths of the gospel and acknowledgment of Christ's authority and lordship. To the post-modern mind these three things — a purposeful plan, absolute or objective truth, and being subject to authority — are the very aspects of modernity which have failed, only leading to the exploitation of mankind and therefore are to be rejected. Herein lies today's challenge for the church in seeking to reach into the heart of the world with the gospel. The great consolation is that it is the Saviour who sends his church into this world, not to be *of* the world but *in* the world.

'My prayer [prays Jesus] is not that you take them [his disciples] out of the world but that you protect them from the evil one. They are not of the world, even as I am not of it. Sanctify them by the truth; your word is truth. As you sent me into the world, I have sent them into the world'

(John 17:15-18).

## Beginning where it may hurt!

Question! Does today's church, or rather each individual claiming the name of Christian, believe that the Great Commission is God's master plan for mankind, based upon the unchanging absolutes of the gospel and giving no alternative for discipleship other than total submission to the lordship of Christ? The question is posed at this point because there are many indications that the church is in need of evangelization, for we are all susceptible to the influence of perpetual bombardment by these 'sacred doctrines' of today's society. This will be addressed in a later chapter, but it is all too evident that today we see both those in the pew, and at times those in the pulpit, wavering under the effects of radical pluralism, individualism and relativism, whereas Jesus calls us to set the agenda by living consistently as 'salt' and 'light' (Matthew 5:13-16), rather than following the agenda set by today's society.

There are lessons to learn from the church in Eastern Europe in this respect. Living through decades where the Communist authorities endeavoured to strip society of any Christian influence, as the changes came, there are many instances of the church thoughtfully addressing the challenge of bringing the Christian ethic and foundation back into people's thinking. Typical is the Mission Statement raised in the new situation by the Free Evangelical Church (Cirkev Bratska) of the Republic of Slovakia which reads as follows:

> *In the midst of uncertainty and spiritual hunger Cirkev Bratska desires — to be a clear expression of God's Person, to work towards personal faith and growth of the individuals in the fellowship and to strive for unity in diversity so that above all, the values of the Gospel of Jesus Christ are instilled into every area of life and society.*

## Salt and light

Now salt is salt and light is light, they can be no other. In whatever environment they find themselves, they cannot be other than what they are and from the text we see that the church is to be the salt of 'the earth' and the light of 'the world'. We are called upon to be no more than salt and light, but equally we are called to be no less. The question then is: 'Where is the church of Jesus Christ?' In posing such a question John Stott goes on to remark:

*Why are the salt and light of Jesus Christ not permeating and changing our society? It is sheer hypocrisy on our part to raise our eyebrows, shrug our shoulders or wring our hands. The Lord Jesus told us to be the world's salt and light. If therefore darkness and rottenness abound, it is our fault and we must accept the blame.* [8]

The church has been placed under an inescapable and compelling obligation and she has been allowed by God to be entrusted with the gospel. In writing to the Thessalonian church the apostle Paul expressed this truth in this way:

…we speak as men approved by God to be entrusted with the gospel

(1 Thessalonians 2:4).

In many ways the world is more open for the gospel than it was when modern-day missions were born. The world has 'shrunk' in a manner that could never have been envisaged by missionaries of the last hundred years. Geographically most places are more readily accessible. Literacy has seen a phenomenal leap forward and linguistically ears and eyes are tuned to all that the media can provide. Add to this, mankind's continuing search for the transcendent, and countless opportunities for proclaiming Christ present themselves. It has been said that the one who picks up an acorn holds a forest in his fist. Such are today's opportunities and potential.

## A sinful and lost world

Once again Petre was keenly absorbing the Bible teaching given in Slavic Gospel Association's Mission School in Bulgaria. This in itself was a great testimony to God's saving and keeping power. Petre is a gypsy pastor and was the channel through whom God worked to establish a Bible-preaching church in the village where he had been known as a drunkard and a wife-beater. On one occasion Petre shared with us how his former life had been such that one day he had reached such a low ebb that he sold his dog for a bucket of alcohol. Petre's eyes filled with tears as he said, '*then the Lord found me* and through his saving grace my life and that of my family has been transformed'.

Jaroslav is a young pastor in the Republic of Slovakia. As with Petre in Bulgaria, Jaroslav is leading a newly-planted local church. Having had a good education, his background was very different from that of Petre. In giving his testimony, Jaroslav often tells how he came to saving faith through the witness of a group of Christian young people. As he says, 'My first prayer was, "*Lord I am like a lost sheep. I cannot find you, so you must find me*" and the Lord graciously heard and answered that prayer.'

The Bible challenges us never to forget that, above all, by nature mankind is lost and perishing, 'dead in transgressions and sins' (Ephesians 2:1). The only remedy that can be found is that of which the apostle Paul writes in Ephesians 2:4-6:

> But because of his great love for us, God, who is rich in mercy, made us alive with Christ even when we were dead in transgressions — it is by grace you have been saved.

Generally, sin and guilt have been redefined by today's society. It is no longer an issue and therefore the concept of 'lostness' and eternal punishment has become blurred. This in turn has impinged itself upon Christian thinking. A great change has come over the evangelical world in the past few decades. Hesitation is shown concerning the question that souls without Christ are perishing. Where do we stand on this matter as we seek to reach into the heart of the world?

Consider the past generations of which few remain. When Amy Carmichael dreamed of a great company of people pouring over a precipice while unconcerned Christians played at making daisy chains nearby, was she out of her mind? When Hudson Taylor agonized in prayer because a million Chinese passed into a Christless eternity every month, or when Wesley, Whitefield, Moody, Spurgeon and a host of others preached on the 'lostness of the soul', were they deluded? We may be moved by the deprived social conditions in which some people are living and as Christians this ought to concern us. We may be rightly horrified by disease and distress that some have to face, but the ultimate challenge must always be the destiny of a man's soul.

When the young, eminent Dr Martin Lloyd-Jones was confronting the question of whether his future should be in medicine or in preaching the gospel, he experienced an event that had a profound effect upon his decision. At the time he was at the famous St Bartholomew's London teaching hospital, working under Sir Thomas Hodder, medical adviser to the monarchy. The incident relates to one of the Chiefs at 'Bart's' standing at the door of Lloyd-Jones' research room and asking if he might come in and sit by his fire. A lady friend to whom this man was closely attached had suddenly died. For some two hours, without a word, the distraught man stared vacantly into the fire, until every aspect of the scene was indelibly fixed upon Lloyd-Jones' memory. In his own words Lloyd-Jones said,

*I saw the vanity of all human greatness. Here was a tragedy, a man without hope at all.*[9]

It was the spiritual condition of the lost that impelled the missionary pioneers of the past to go out and endure so much and often to lay down their lives. William Carey wrote:

> *In order to be prepared for our great and solemn work, it is absolutely necessary that we set infinite value upon immortal souls. If we have not this sense of the value of souls, it is impossible that we can feel aright in any other part of our work, and in this case it had been better for us to have been in any other situation than that of a missionary.*

## The crises of life!

Calvin Millar suggests that there are six basic questions that every generation raises:

> *What is the purpose of life?*
> *What am I doing here?*
> *How did I come to be?*
> *Where will I end up?*
> *How can I be happy, or happier?*
> *What does it mean to be human?*[10]

These questions normally show themselves in one form or another, as people face what are thought of as the four major crises of life: namely, birth and bereavement, family relationships, illness and economic pressures. Therefore if we are to minister the gospel into a broken world we will best do that by addressing people where they are, rather than where we think they ought to be, or where we long for them to be. Assuming Millar's assessment of questioning generations is correct, our assurance is that the gospel confronts every one of those questions and does so in a manner that will find its practical outworking as people face the inevitable crises of life.

## The good news that really is good news!

In a slightly rearranged order, consider how the six questions to which we have referred find an answer in the gospel we proclaim.

### 1.  *How did I come to be?*

> Then God said, 'Let us make man in our image, in our likeness…'
>
> (Genesis 1:26).

To be able to fully understand how man is like God, we would need the capacity to totally comprehend the essence and nature of God. This is where the finite mind struggles to grasp the infinite, but what we can say is that as with God, man has a spiritual, moral, mental, relational and immortal dimension. Sadly sin distorted that image of God in man.

> '…God made mankind upright, but men have gone in search of many schemes'
>
> (Ecclesiastes 7:29).

Consequently, the true image of God in man can only be seen in the earthly life of Christ — the sinless one. Therefore the only possibility that man has to reflect that image of God is through a living relationship with Christ Jesus.

## 2.  *What am I doing here and what is the purpose of life?*

The first question in the *Westminster Larger Catechism* is 'What is the chief and highest end of man?' The answer is, 'Man's chief and highest end is to glorify God, and fully to enjoy him for ever.' God did not and could not need to create man to make himself more complete, for he is uniquely complete in himself. God speaks of his sons and daughters from the ends of the earth as those 'whom I created for my glory' (Isaiah 43:7). Therefore, we are to 'do all to the glory of God' (1 Corinthians 10:31). The fact that God created man guarantees that our lives have significance and are meaningful, because this is an indication that we are important to God himself.

> 'You are worthy, our Lord and God,
>     to receive glory and honour and power,
> for you created all things,
>     and by your will they were created
>     and have their being'
>
> (Revelation 4:11).

## 3.  *What does it mean to be human?*

*A number of non-Christian [\*and anti-Christian] philosophers have vigorously challenged the idea that man has any immaterial part at all, such as a soul or spirit. Scripture is very clear that we do have a soul as distinct from our physical bodies, which not only can function somewhat independently of our ordinary thought processes (1 Corinthians 14:14; Romans 8:16) but also, when we die, is able to go on consciously acting and relating to God, apart from our physical bodies. Jesus told the dying thief, 'today you will be with Me in Paradise.' (Luke 23:43).*[11]

To ensure that man could live in relationship with his Creator, both through time and eternity, God created man uniquely with body and soul.

(* Author's added comment)

### 4. *How can I be happy?*

> You have made known to me the path of life;
>> you will fill me with joy in your presence,
>> with eternal pleasures at your right hand
>
> (Psalm 16:11).

When a man lives as the Creator intended he is sure to live a fulfilled and satisfied life, Christ Jesus being the channel through which this is possible.

> For in Christ all the fulness of the Deity lives in bodily form, and you have been given fulness in Christ, who is the Head over every power and authority
>
> (Colossians 2:9-10).

### 5. *Where will I end up?*

The Scriptures show clearly that everyone will face judgement — both believers and unbelievers (Romans 2:5-7; Ecclesiastes 12:14; Romans 14:10, 12; 2 Corinthians 5:10).

Although God's punishment of sin serves as a deterrent against further sinning and a warning to those who observe it, primarily God must punish sin, because his own righteousness demands it. However, his mercy provided the one who takes the place of the sinner — even his Son Christ Jesus.

Bearing shame and scoffing rude
In my place condemned He stood,
Sealed my pardon with His blood,
Hallelujah — what a Saviour![12]

## 6. Confidence in the gospel!

J. H. Bavinck writes:

> …it became customary in the literature of international missions
> to speak of 'the four-dimensional character' of missions. Mission,
> so it is held, is simultaneously preaching, education, medical
> care and social-economic aid … this is misleading, for it co-
> ordinated the preaching of the Gospel with education, medical
> care and technical and social economic aid, and it does it in a
> manner that these four things appear to be of equal value, whereas
> Christ actually has only commanded us to preach the Gospel to
> all nations… We have seen that Scripture plainly teaches that
> 'he who is in Christ Jesus is a new creation so that old things are
> passed away and all is become new' (2 Corinthians 5:17) … this
> is our sole concern, and all the other services are meaningful to
> the degree that they assist, clarify or render possible the preaching
> of the Gospel. The missionary approach is therefore not four
> dimensional; it is simple, and its singularity touches life in all
> its aspects.[13]

Maybe not everyone will agree with Bavinck in this respect,
but his assessment pushes each of us to ask ourselves whether
we truly believe that the gospel is all-sufficient in answering
man's deepest questions and reaching into the heart of a broken
world.

# 8.
# Trends or tragedy

It was a beautiful spring evening as we joined the crowds making their way to the local football stadium. The streets were awash with people all heading in the same direction. Young and old seemed to be moving with a quickened step and a buzz of excitement and expectation filled the air.

Romania had seen dramatic changes following the fall of Communism in the previous December of 1989. It was now mid-May 1990 in Oradea, a city situated near the border with Hungary. This was to be the first open-air mass rally that Romanian Christians had known since the new freedoms of religious expression had become possible. Remembering the role of the police during the days of Communism and having had a number of firsthand encounters with them over the years, it was an unreal experience to see friendly and smiling members of the local police directing the masses of people into the stadium. Long before the meeting began, a crowd of around thirty thousand had gathered. A huge white cross towered above the massed choir, which framed the platform, and the brass band that had been assembled from a number of village churches was enthusiastically playing the familiar 'songs of Zion'. As the meeting opened up, it was a vivid reminder of what God had done in making such a witness possible in a country where only a few months earlier the Christians had known intense persecution. However, the reasoning behind using probably the most able Romanian preacher simply to translate the guest speaker — a western evangelist of international renown — seemed distinctly odd. The preaching was followed by the obligatory 'appeal' and many responded by going forward. Because God sovereignly uses what he will, no doubt that evening many were caused to consider their spiritual situation and standing before him.

Within forty-five minutes of the conclusion of the meeting most had left the stadium, but a group of around ten Romanian brothers began speaking with us. These were lay-pastors and church workers we knew well, as part of the unofficial Bible-teaching programme in which Slavic Gospel Association had been involved over previous years. The fading light revealed a quizzical look on their faces as they posed the question: 'Brother, although in many ways this was a wonderful evening, what is it that causes us some unease?' My response was to turn the question back to them in terms of, 'Well, you tell me.' Vasile was never short of a question during the teaching programmes and now he responded again on behalf of the group. 'After tonight's meeting finished,' he said, 'we have been talking together and our concern is that throughout all the evening we never heard the word "repentance". This makes us ask — to what were the people responding?'

This was not a surprising reaction because, for years, the believers in Romania had long carried the name of 'the repenters' as a derogatory title, given to them by Romanian society. However, I felt that Vasile and the other brothers had 'hit the nail on the head'. Certainly the preaching had majored on man's needs rather than God's requirements and one has to question whether a person can truly respond to the gospel of God's grace without repenting of sin. Is a gospel that omits the reality of the need for repentance the true gospel? But this is only the tip of a twenty-first-century iceberg and maybe we have not yet seen the full harvest that comes from the kind of message that we are frequently communicating to the world.

## Danger — 'man' at work!

As John MacArthur comments:

> *If church history teaches us anything, it teaches us that the most devastating assaults on the faith have always begun as subtle errors arising from within the body itself... We minister to people desperate for answers, and we cannot soft-peddle the truth or extenuate the Gospel... If we trust in worldly devices, we automatically relinquish the power of the Holy Spirit.*[1]

A vital question in relation to the Great Commission is 'How do we define success?' About one hundred years ago pragmatism was first popularized as a philosophical lifestyle; that is, 'If it works — it must be good.' Pragmatism has its roots in secular humanism and defines truth as that which is 'useful', 'meaningful' and 'helpful'. Those so-called truths that do not appear to be workable or relevant are disregarded and put to one side. The danger in 'gospel work' is in attempting to meet the demands of human nature for success and, in trying to feed this syndrome, we are drawn increasingly in this direction. There are tangible evidences that this has invaded today's Christian thinking particularly when the gospel appears to be making little or no impact. We readily run to ask whether God's work is successful, rather than first questioning whether it is biblical. It is reckoned that currently, worldwide, fifty new congregations are established each week by the Jehovah's Witness organization. What could be more 'successful' than this? But the reality is that the Jehovah's Witness teachings are not biblical.

Mary Slessor (1848-1915), that great lady missionary to Calabar (known as the 'white man's grave' in West Africa), had a very straightforward approach to ministry and expressed it with the words: 'Christ sent me to preach the gospel and he will look after the results.' We are all aware of the pressures faced by the overseas missionary to 'produce the goods', as they send their prayer letters to their supporting churches or donors. Such pressures have caused some to give up because of a sense of failure, and this is a reality that has not only been faced by the overseas missionary. The temptation to do exactly this caused Kent Hughes to go into print on this whole subject with the telling title *Liberating Ministry from the Success Syndrome*. In this he wrote:

> We are concerned about the morale and survival of those in Christian ministry. Pastors, youth workers, evangelists, Sunday school teachers, lay pastors, missionaries, Bible study leaders, Christian writers and speakers and those in other areas of Christian service, who often face significant feelings of failure, usually fuelled by misguided expectations for success.[2]

This approach of 'softening' the gospel and meeting the demands for success appear to have the same root; namely that of primarily meeting man's needs using man-made methods, rather than prioritizing with God's requirements, person and essence, as revealed in his Word. Of course, we ought to expect the gospel of Jesus Christ to have good success but certain things are not negotiable. The Lord assured Joshua that he

'will be prosperous and successful', but this had a condition
attached to it:

> 'Do not let this Book of the Law depart from your
> mouth; meditate on it day and night, so that you may be
> careful to do everything written in it'
>
> (Joshua 1:8).

Equally, Nehemiah was a man who asked God to give him
success, but he did so as one who came prayerfully in awe of
his God.

> 'O Lord, let your ear be attentive to the prayer of this
> your servant ... who delight[s] in revering your name.
> Give your servant success today...'
>
> (Nehemiah 1:11).

The word translated as 'revering' literally means 'to fear from
apprehension of danger and with a sense of our own weakness'.[3]
This tells us a great deal about Nehemiah's heart as he seeks
success, as opposed to the pragmatic approach adopted by
so much of today's evangelism and missionary enterprise.
Ultimately, this can only work against the Great Commission
rather than enhancing it. The apostle Paul explained why he
was constrained to write the letter to the Galatians:

> I am astonished that you are so quickly deserting the one
> who called you by the grace of Christ and are turning to
> a different gospel — which is really no gospel at all.

He continues:

Am I now trying to win the approval of men, or of God?
Or am I trying to please men? If I were still trying to
please men, I would not be a servant of Christ
                                                    (Galatians 1:6, 10).

In the case of the Galatians the problem was a message of the
'gospel plus' but, equally, omissions from the gospel of grace
cause it to be 'no gospel at all' and here, for example, I take
you back to the words of our Romanian brothers mentioned
earlier, '...we never heard the word "repentance". This makes
us ask — to what were the people responding?'

## The user-friendly gospel?

At a conference in the UK in November 2003 Dr Paul
Negrut, Romanian pastor, international preacher and leader
in the Baptist church of Romania, addressed the question of
today's approach in understanding and facing the challenge
of the Christian gospel. He gave the conference one of two
alternatives as he said, 'You have a choice. You can have your
theology derived "from below" or "from above".' With that
simple phrase he summarized the two major approaches we
see at play in today's world scene. He then went on to make it
clear from where he believed our theology should derive: 'from
above'.

Theology rooted 'from below' usually begins with the
argument that the world is either post-Christian, anti-Christian
and/or post-modern. Therefore, for the Christian message to
make a connection, it must first and foremost address man's
needs and this becomes the channel through which men and
women will begin to hear what the Bible has to say. Sadly, the

last few decades have proved that this emphasis has produced a self-centred type of 'believer' where, above everything else, God is there to satisfy my need. At our peril, the teaching we have again and again in Scripture concerning the Lordship of Christ and the bondservant picture[4] of the true Christian has been negated as being too harsh and one which will drive people away. This in turn has developed the idea that a Christian is one who is his own man, with control over his own life, having the right to make his choices and to insist on his rights. Bible texts such as 1 Corinthians 6:19-20: 'You are not your own; you were bought at a price'; and Mark 8:34, where Jesus says, 'If anyone would come after me, he must deny himself and take up his cross and follow me', have become a low priority. Who in their right mind would respond to such a message, for this is certainly not user-friendly?

In a very subtle change in evangelical terminology we now hear of people 'making a commitment' to Christ rather than surrendering their lives to him; or 'coming to know God' rather than seeking God's forgiveness and repenting of one's sins. Could it be that this is an indicator and a warning that the time has come to redress the balance and, by God's good grace, make it our aim to spread a 'gospel theology' that is God-centred and comes from above?

Pastor Paul Mallard, the incoming president of the UK Fellowship of Independent Evangelical Churches (F.I.E.C.), posed a question in the Autumn 2003 F.I.E.C. magazine[5]: 'Where are all the pastors?' In answering the question he gave many helpful and challenging thoughts but I would suggest that part of the answer, at least, is that we are seeing the results of a man-centred gospel and we could equally ask, 'Where are the church workers and lay leaders?' or, 'Where are the missionaries?'

A number of years ago an advertisement appeared in a London newspaper which produced a remarkable response. It read:

> Men wanted for hazardous journey, small wages, bitter cold, long months of complete darkness, constant danger, safe return doubtful. Honour and recognition in the event of success.

It seems that thousands of men responded because the advertisement was signed by the world-famous Arctic explorer, Sir Ernest Shackleton. This was not very user-friendly but Shackleton's signature made all the difference.

The Lord Jesus is the greatest and most gracious Master anyone could be called upon to serve, but to accomplish eternal results that glorify God, it must be on his terms.


## Sh...sh — keep it quiet!

The great missionary movement of the nineteenth century not only carried the deep conviction that without the gospel people cannot be saved, but they also earnestly believed that the Scriptures clearly teach of conscious eternal punishment for those who die outside of Christ. Inevitably a gospel where this teaching is downplayed will undermine the urgency which is a vital part of the Great Commission. The trend has been to ignore parts of Scripture such as Luke 16:19-31 (the parable of Lazarus and the rich man); Revelation 20:11-15 (the book of life and the lake of fire); Matthew 25:41-46 (the separation of the righteous from the unrighteous); and other similar passages. These teachings are looked on as 'being in bad taste' and not quite the thing to talk about, yet as John MacArthur points out:

> *the most prolific teacher on hell in all of the Scripture was the Lord Jesus Himself. He had more to say about the subject than all the apostles, prophets and evangelists of Scripture put together.*[6]

The consequence of attempting to lower the profile of Bible teaching on eternal punishment inevitably means that other explanations have to be found, because eternal issues are certainly there in the Bible and as evangelicals 'we believe in the Bible'. So today we find some Christian preachers and leaders who would carry the label 'evangelical' wavering on this issue by suggesting, or even teaching, other alternatives; and an unclear sound echoes out. This is basically showing itself in one of three fashionable theological stances 'from below'; namely, universalism, annihilationism and conditional immortality. Briefly, these can be defined as follows:

- *Universalism* is the view that insists that God's mercy is such that he will eventually draw and win all men to himself because inherent in man is that which drives him Godward.
- *Annihilationism* teaches that although all souls are immortal and God must judge everyone because of his righteousness, God's love forbids the concept of eternal suffering, therefore the punishment of the soul of the unsaved person will be an obliteration into nothingness.
- *Conditional immortality* holds that man's soul is not inherently immortal. Therefore the final judgement will give immortality to the righteous, while the unsaved will be deprived of this and pass into oblivion as God's judgement. Of course,

this is 'nothing new under the sun'. Jonathan Edwards, who preached to great effect a remarkable sermon entitled 'Sinners in the Hands of an Angry God' at Enfield on 8 July 1741, stated:

*It is strange how men will go directly against so plain and full revelations of Scripture as to suppose, notwithstanding all these things, that the eternal punishment threatened against the wicked signifies no more than annihilation.*[7]

Finally, this question of eternal punishment can only be resolved by reference to the Scriptures. I submit that for the Evangelical Church to regain the zeal for fulfilling the mandate of the Great Commission, it will need to rediscover the truth of eternal punishment, rather than deny it, and then proclaim once more this sombre Bible teaching, with heartfelt compassion and even tears.

## All roads lead to...???

Another marked trend which calls for consideration is the tendency to reduce Christian mission to influencing society with Christian values rather than giving a clear proclamation of Christ's unique atoning, redeeming and saving work. We live in a multi-faith world and the UK is becoming increasingly a multi-faith society where Christianity is considered to be only one faith among many. This pluralistic approach in the UK is exemplified by the fact that Prince Charles, the heir to the throne who, in succession, would hold the position of head of the Anglican Church and bear the title 'Defender of The Faith', has made it clear that he would consider himself to be defender of faiths rather than promoting one faith. We have now moved into a UK scenario where the Christian faith stands only as one valid option among many and to insist that Christ is the only way to God is considered to be not only politically unacceptable, but intellectually arrogant and lacking in love and compassion. Interestingly, neither Islam, Judaism or Buddhism permits the concept of pluralism in their differing fundamental teachings, even though some adherents may say the contrary.

No Christian who takes the Great Commission seriously can simultaneously align with pluralism because the mandate is to 'disciple the nations', which is a far greater concept than simply bringing individuals to him. The implication is one of reaching into people groups, which not only have a perceived sense of their own identity in terms of their culture, but also their religious beliefs. How are the 'nations to be discipled'? As Jesus said:

'[by] teaching them to obey everything I have commanded you'

(Matthew 28:20).

As evangelical Christians we have to be the first to admit that we do not have all the answers to every question that arises from taking the gospel into all the world, but the Bible does not permit us to see man's salvation as possible through any other means than the sacrificial death of the only Son of God, Jesus Christ. As the evangelical Christian world flirts with pluralism, it inevitably leads to the erosion of the uniqueness of Christ and that in turn undermines the authority of Scripture. Consequently, this has led many evangelical churches and mission agencies to re-focus on relief or 'compassion' ministries, rather than overt evangelism or church-planting. Of course, we know that practical helps are vital in many areas of our society and in the world at large, but again we return to the question of the priorities spoken of by our Lord in the Great Commission. One measure of current Christian thinking is shown in that it is far easier to raise funds to assist a widow in Eastern Europe through the winter than it is to support a national Christian in a church-planting ministry, when in reality we ought to be able to do both. Or again, funds will flood in to build an orphanage in a deprived part of the world, but to find financial support for a Bible translator proves to be far more difficult.

## Doom and gloom? Not at all!

These are days of enormous possibilities and potential. As Peskett and Ramchandra remind us:[8]

> in his farewell address to the Ephesian church leaders at Miletus, the apostle Paul reminds them how 'he testified to both Jews and Greeks about repentance towards God and faith towards our Lord Jesus' (Acts 20:21) and that he 'did not shrink from declaring to you the whole purpose of God' (Acts 20:27). Such a comprehensive ministry springs from a comprehensive grasp of the Gospel. In the letter to that same church, Paul writes of the 'one new humanity' that God has created through the cross of Christ (Ephesians 2:15) and how mission throughout the Gentile world is to make plain to everyone the administration (plan) of this mystery, which for ages past was kept hidden in God, Who created all things. His intent was that now, through the Church, the manifold wisdom of God should be made known to the rulers and authorities in the heavenly realms (Ephesians 3:9-10).

It has been said that people are driven from the Christian church, not so much by stern truth that makes them uneasy, but by weak nothings that make them contemptuous. Jesus was quite clear in his teaching on this matter.

> And he who does not take up his cross and follow Me [cleave steadfastly to Me, conforming wholly to My example in living and, if need be, in dying also] is not worthy of Me. Whoever finds his [lower] life will lose it [the higher life], and whoever loses his [lower] life on My account will find it [the higher life]
> (Matthew 10:38-39, The Amplified Bible).

Our Saviour left no middle ground in the gospel he preached. Spare your life or sacrifice your life. Nothing could be more definite than this. In Matthew 10, the verses preceding those quoted above identify what the probable costs will be and this is not a comfortable message. But we have the assurance that if we are forever protecting our own interests, we will lose. Conversely, if we die to self and live for Christ, we gain.

In a world of uncertainty and doubt, is the church of Jesus Christ presenting a message that carries such clarity? Do those around us 'hear' this as the Christian gospel, as portrayed by our lives?

# 9.
# When will we ever learn?

*On 9th January, 1985, the steel door of Sofia's Central Prison
closed behind me with resounding finality.*[1]

So begins the story of Hristo Kulichev, an evangelical pastor in
the days of Communist Bulgaria, imprisoned for his refusal to
submit to the authorities who sought to prevent him preaching
the gospel. He continues:

*I would soon be locked in a cell with men who were common
criminals. This was the beginning of three and one-half years
when every movement and activity, indeed my very life, was
rigidly controlled by the agents of a repressive atheistic regime.
Arrested for preaching Christ and the freedom to worship under
His authority, those years were a difficult time for me as well as
for my family. But in the midst of the difficulty God sustained us
with His grace and taught us some of the most valuable lessons
of our lives.*

Recalling one occasion in the early period of that imprisonment,
Hristo speaks of the day he spent with his brother Dimitar,
who was also detained for a short time.

*It was on my fortieth day in prison that the footsteps led again to the door of my cell. Summoned to follow the guard into the reception area of Sofia's Central Prison, I wondered what lay ahead. As long as I live, I'll never forget seeing Dimitar there and being allowed to speak with him alone… We were placed in a cell with one small window, but the glass in it was broken, allowing the cold winter winds to penetrate the cell. If you check the records, you'll see that the winter of '85 in Sofia was a cold one, and that night was among the coldest. It made little difference to my brother and me, however. Like Paul and Silas in the prison in Philippi, we spent the night sharing and singing and praising God…*

*Dimitar told me of his witness among the prisoners. One of his cell mates was a man named Assen, who seemed to be searching for spiritual guidance. I promised to pray for Assen and told Dimitar of those I was witnessing to as well.*

*We reaffirmed our commitment to stand firm for our faith in Jesus Christ and renewed our resolve to serve Him no matter what the cost… We sang an entire concert of hymns and Christian songs that cold night…Our hearts were overflowing with thankfulness. Neither of us felt we were in the Central Prison in Sofia. It was as though we were in heaven, singing with the angels themselves… By remaining true to Christ's command not to be ashamed of Him (Luke 9:26), we discovered greater depths of God's grace and mercy than either of us had thought possible.*

The history of the church of Jesus Christ is strewn with such testimonies as we follow its successes and failures in carrying out Christ's Great Commission to 'go into all the world and preach the gospel to every creature', and 'disciple the nations'. I was privileged to know Hristo and his family a number of years before his imprisonment and was frequently challenged by his unbending desire to serve his Lord, come what may. On one occasion, about eighteen months before his arrest, I will never forget the moving manner in which he and his dear wife Tzvete shared something of their testimony with us. They talked of the time when they first knew the call of God into pastoral ministry. Hristo said, 'That night we knelt in prayer together and prayed that by God's grace, we would be faithful to him at all times, no matter what the cost.'

There is no doubt that their firm stand was used of God to fuel the spread of the gospel throughout Bulgaria, when the days of opportunity came following Gorbachev's *glasnost*[2] and *perestroika*[3] in 1988, leading to the 1989 fall of Communism. It is not without significance that Hristo and Dimitar sang praises to their Lord, as did Paul and Silas in the days of the New Testament church. The great story upon which today's church is built is one of how the Spirit-anointed band of previously faltering disciples began by going at Christ's call, having the assurance of his promise that he would build his church. They simply went out to preach the gospel in spite of tremendous opposition, an opposition that was to span the centuries.

It has been said on more than one occasion that the only thing we appear to learn from history is that 'we never seem to learn from history'. Yet there is so much to be gained by considering those historical influences and trends which have worked for or against the Great Commission. As A. M. Renwick has commented:

> To help guide our steps aright in the present we must know something of the past: and if the Church of God is to escape today the nemesis which always follows certain lines of action, she must learn to ponder carefully the experiences of other days, whether these were good or evil.[4]

## The early years

There is a great deal of authenticated literary information that relates to the history of the New Testament church, the best of these being the New Testament writings themselves. What emerges is that during the two hundred and fifty years after Pentecost the church experienced times of sporadic and sometimes severe persecution, but still the church grew and spread, making its home in an ever-widening circle of cultures and contexts. While in some places this brought intensified opposition, at other times and in other locations the church tended to be appreciated, growing in influence and even increasing in prestige, wealth and comfort. Along the north coast of Africa the churches multiplied robustly. To the west, the Christian faith became firmly established in Spain and Italy. Further north small Christian communities came into being in Gaul — today's France — and Germany and Britain. The significance of this was that it signalled the growth of the church beyond the fringes of the Roman Empire and the Greek-speaking world. To the east, today's Iran, Armenia, Ethiopia and India were all experiencing Christian churches being planted. This indicates that by one route or another many Christians, in addition to the Apostles, must have intentionally travelled past the comfort zone of a familiar culture and language, and the relative safety of Rome's stabilizing influence.

## Suffering and persecution

The incredible spread of the gospel of Jesus Christ was not without cost and, inevitably, whereas the earliest persecution of Christians had come from the hands of the Jews, during the second and third centuries it came from the pagan world of the day. There were many devotees of the vast array of pantheon deities and other philosophies that warred for the minds of the masses, alongside situations where corrupt means of gaining wealth were attacked by the impact of the gospel. Christ had warned his disciples, 'If they persecuted me, they will persecute you also' (John 15:20), and this became a daily reality for many 'ordinary' believers. Early historians and Christian apologists record many of the events of the day in their extra-biblical writings.[5] The first great Roman persecution came around AD 64 when the Emperor Nero, who had lost all reputation and was believed to be the author of a series of calamities that were falling on Rome, caused the Christians to be blamed for the great fire of Rome. Through this, Christianity became a hated 'sect'. Nero even offered his gardens for the spectacle of crucified Christians, whose bodies were covered with wax and other combustible materials, being set on fire to serve as lights to illuminate the night skies. Such persecutions quickly spread throughout the Roman Empire.

Nero's death and the fall of Jerusalem brought some respite from such things, but a resurgence of intense suffering came at the close of the first century towards the end of Emperor Domitian's reign. Using the charge of atheism, he caused many Christians to be put to death because of their refusal to worship the pagan gods. Yet the gospel continued to spread. The patient heroism of multitudes of Christians under cruel persecution attested to the fact of a faith grounded in the living Christ and a gospel of eternal value. The oft-quoted phrase of Tertullian, 'the blood of the martyrs was the seed of the Church' was the reality of the day.

By the middle of the second century the early apologist Justin Martyr was writing:

*There is not one single race of men, whether barbarians or Greeks, or whatever they may be called, nomads or vagrants, or herdsmen living in tents, among whom prayers and giving thanks are not offered through the name of the crucified Christ.*[6]

Against the background of heathen immorality, the character and example of Christians became like a beacon of light that was undeniable. This caused Tertullian to write of the Christian testimony:

*We have filled every place among you* ['*you*' being the heathen society of the day], *– cities, islands, fortresses, towns, market places … senate, forum, – we have left nothing to you but the temples of your gods. Were the Christians to retire from the heathen community, you would be horror struck at the solitude in which you would find yourselves… You would have to seek subjects to govern. You would have more enemies than citizens remaining.*[7]

*Ever since the Church's first great conflict with the power of imperial Rome, the victory of the Gospel has been won, not by the efficiency of its mission strategists, the effectiveness of its fund-raisers or even the cleverness of its preachers, but by the blood of its martyrs.*[8]

This truism can be traced down the centuries through to today. What lessons follow from these events and situations concerning the Great Commission? I suggest that at least four facts are very evident.

1.  For the spread of the gospel a suffering or persecuted church is the norm and not the exception. This is clearly indicated in

both the Scriptures and in the history of the people of God. Not that we seek suffering or persecution, but that we are not caught by surprise when it comes. The apostle Paul, writing as one who suffered much, reminds us:

> In fact, everyone who wants to live a godly life in Christ Jesus will be persecuted
>
> (2 Timothy 3:12).

and the apostle Peter adds from his experience:

> But even if you should suffer for what is right, you are blessed
>
> (1 Peter 3:14).

2. When suffering or persecution comes, the ones who are previously fully surrendered to Christ become more convinced in their walk and witness, while those who are not, find great difficulty in standing firm.

There appears to be a mode of thinking which comes to the conclusion that persecution *automatically* strengthens the church or the individual Christian. History tends not to validate this thought. For example, as the Eastern European countries were swept under the heel of atheistic communism in the mid/late 1940s it seems that, in general, those who had not 'meant business' with God beforehand were washed away, whilst those who bore a clear testimony of life prior to the persecution became stronger in their witness. Recall again, as previously mentioned, what Hristo and Tzvete Kulichev prayed years before imprisonment came. The matter was settled on their knees with God long before Hristo was brought before his accusers.

3. A suffering church that faithfully stands firm communicates the gospel to a lost world in a manner that is not only powerful but also unique. In his prison letter to the Colossians Paul writes:

> Now I rejoice in what was suffered for you, and I fill up in my flesh what is still lacking in regard to Christ's afflictions[9], for the sake of his body, which is the church (1:24).

Paul is speaking from the closeness he feels to his precious Jesus, his Lord and Saviour. He is reflecting on the affliction which the Saviour, the Suffering Servant, endured during his earthly ministry in order to reveal the love of God in all its fulness to a lost world. Now the Apostle associates himself, the church as the body of Christ, and consequently every believer, with this same ministry. This is the unique privilege afforded to every believer through which the reaction to suffering can be a powerful 'preached' message to the world.

4. Consider it pure joy, my brothers, whenever you face trials of many kinds.

So writes James as he opens his Epistle (1:2) and in doing so he echoes a remarkable intertwining theme of Scripture — that of suffering accompanied by joy, or expressed in another way, persecution adjoined to glory. This is beyond all reason and rationale, for how can suffering bring joy? In response, Scripture gives us the supreme example in the Lord Jesus Christ:

> …who for *the joy* set before him endured *the cross*, scorning its shame, and sat down at the right hand of the throne of God. Consider him who endured such opposition

from sinful men, so that you will not grow weary and
lose heart

(Hebrews 12:2-3).

As E. H. Broadbent says, as he writes in *The Pilgrim Church*:

*The first three centuries of the Church's history prove that no
earthly power can crush it. It is invincible to attacks from without.
The witnesses of its sufferings, and even its persecutors become
its converts and it grows more rapidly than it can be destroyed.*[10]

The following modern-day account from Eastern Europe is a
typical example.

*In the days of Communism Nadia was a problem to the Romanian
authorities. She travelled into the surrounding villages to visit
and help elderly people. In a land where Bibles were in short
supply her question to us was always the same: 'Have you any
large print Bibles for my old people?' Nadia's activities eventually
led to a raid on her home by the police that brought with it an
accompanying house search. On a subsequent meeting with
Nadia we asked about that experience.*

*'Well, yes,' she replied, 'it was difficult. Six policemen spent
seven hours in our home, searching and questioning, questioning
and searching. They confiscated my English Bible that I loved
so much and seemed convinced that I had huge quantities of
Romanian Bibles hidden in the house. This has never been so and
I assured them of this, but they were not convinced.' In an almost
detached way she continued to tell how at one point they tapped
the walls, and finding one place sounding hollow, tore away the
plaster. 'There was nothing there, of course', she said, 'only the
crumbling plaster of my old cottage.'*

*'Nadia', we said, 'you know that believers back home have prayed for you and your ministry. How should we ask them to pray now?' She glanced knowingly into our eyes with a look that read our thoughts. We were feeling sorry for her and she knew it. With the index finger of her right hand raised, she emphasized what she was about to tell us.*

*'Now look here,' she said with that patient, understanding tone we had come to know so well, 'we do need your prayers but not your pity.' She continued, 'First we should praise the Lord together. The Lord is so gracious and kind. He really must love me very much to trust me with such an experience. Now I know beyond all doubt that I am precious to Him.'*

*Then with that twinkle in the eye caught from her elderly mother she said, 'Brother, sister, think how good the Lord is. He sent six policemen to my home for seven hours so that I could tell them of my Saviour's love. Maybe they would never have heard in any other way.' Then as an impish smile unfolded across her face she said, 'They were a captive audience, they just would not go away.'*[11]

## The problems of growth!

Following Pentecost, as Peter preaches in Jerusalem, the crowds are gripped with the conviction of sin and are caused to cry out to Peter and the rest, 'Brothers, what shall we do?' (Acts 2:37). Peter's ready response is 'Repent and be baptized' and around three thousand were added to the church that day. These were people who became Christians not in name only, but by life and practice. 'And the Lord added to their number daily those who were being saved' (Acts 2:47). Within a short space of time 'many who heard the message believed, and the number of men grew to about five thousand' (Acts 4:4).

This rapid numerical enlargement of the church in Jerusalem, consisting partly of native and partly of foreign Jews who used the Greek language, soon ran into a problem. The Grecian Jews, also known as the Hellenists, felt that in the daily supply for the poor, the Apostles had not ministered equal relief to their widows. With a thoughtful and wise response, the Apostles led the whole church into appointing seven deacons to take care of this matter (Acts 6:5:6). Interestingly, all seven who were appointed had a Grecian name. 'So the word of God spread. The number of disciples in Jerusalem increased rapidly, and a large number of priests became obedient to the faith' (Acts 6:7).

Now, as the gospel was carried from Jerusalem into the Gentile world, it found a ready response there. This caused the Jewish Christians great concern. Their attachment to their own religious roots and national peculiarities saw them calling for the Gentile converts to comply with the whole of the Mosaic Law in order to know salvation in all its fulness. This appears to be the first time that man's natural pride, disguised under the pretence of religious zeal, attempted to undermine the simplicity of the faith which up to now had rested on trust in Jesus alone and obedience to his word. So we see that before the close of the first century the Great Commission came under serious threat, not so much from external pressures, but *from within the church itself*. Thankfully the Spirit of God prevailed as Paul, Barnabas and Peter gave ample proof of God's divine grace extended to the Gentile world. Although, having said that, it cannot be without significance that the time came when God saw fit to move the missionary-sending centre of the day from

Jerusalem to Antioch. Was it that Jerusalem's pride in who it was became overshadowed by Antioch's zeal in fulfilling what it was called to do?

However, the great Gentile debate of that first Jerusalem Council signalled a problem which has dogged the church to this present day, for as the church grew in size and geographical location, two questions became ever more pressing. How could the church keep all the scattered parts in a unity with each other? And how could the church be kept from being subverted by heresy from within? These were, and always will be, difficult issues to resolve and the manner in which they are resolved will greatly affect the church's attitude to the mandate carried in the Great Commission.

What appears to have happened in the case of the church as it moved into the second century, with the Apostles now all with the Lord, is that it began to be taken up with its organizational structure and with administration, which inevitably caused it to become increasingly concerned with internal matters.

What evolved was that the very councils whose purpose it was to resolve questions and differences by agreeing on teaching and practice became the places where disagreements became entrenched. This, in turn, gave birth to divisions and factions where, increasingly, the Great Commission was taken from the hands of the 'ordinary' disciple and became the concern of the clergy and the slippery slope of dependence on authoritarian control was set in place. Even Aurelius Augustine (354-430), who stood so firm against Pelagian teaching[12] by insisting that sin wrought such ravages in man that he could not save himself and who has been referred to as 'the greatest Christian of his age', taught that there was no salvation outside the visible Catholic Church — a church already bound by traditionalism and sacramentarianism.

The Church's one foundation
Is Jesus Christ her Lord;
She is His new creation
By water and the Word;
From heaven He came and sought her
To be His holy bride
With His own blood He bought her,
And for her life He died.

Though with a scornful wonder
Men see her sore oppressed,
By schisms rent asunder,
By heresies distressed,
Yet saints their watch are keeping,
Their cry goes up, 'How long?'
And soon the night of weeping
Shall be the morn of song.

(Samuel John Stone, 1839-1900)

## The plague of popularity!

In the year AD 305 two Caesars — Constantius in the West and Galerius in the East — took the rule of the Empire, and whilst Constantius was more favourable to the Christian cause, Galerius raged with unchecked fury against the followers of Christ. Within a few years both Constantius and Galerius had died. Constantius was succeeded by his son Constantine and the army acknowledged him as Emperor of the West.

On 28 October AD 312 in the strife that followed, Constantine won a famous victory at the battle of Milvian Bridge against Maxentius who had seized the government of

Africa and Italy. A direct result of this was that a decree was issued from Milan in March AD 313 giving full toleration to the Christian faith, ordering that all places of worship taken from the Christians should be restored without delay; that any loss they had suffered should be made good; and that Christian leaders should be released from any municipal offices which might detract from their ministry. Almost overnight this brought about a startling change to the circumstances and standing of every Christian in the empire and was to be the first of several edicts which ended in the establishment of Christianity as the religion of the empire.

This miraculous turn of events is attributed by Eusebius to a miraculous conversion to Christianity by Constantine. Eusebius relates that on his way to engage in the battle of Milvian Bridge, Constantine saw a cross, suspended above the sun and surrounded by the phrase 'Conquer in This'.[13] This was interpreted to Constantine in a vision during the night following, in which Christ stood before him with this same sign, commanding it to be emblazoned upon the shields and standards of the whole army. Various views have been expressed about whether Constantine's 'conversion experience' was genuine, simply a dream or rather more subtly, politically convenient. Whatever it may have been, the effects were far reaching for the Christians and no one can criticize them for grasping with both hands such respite from the severe persecution that had been their lot for so long. Christians could now meet openly without fear of harassment. Sundays became holidays affording the opportunity to meet for worship and fellowship. Money was showered upon them by Constantine to multiply copies of the New Testament writings and provision was made to support the clergy by the State. It was like heaven on earth ... or was it?

Many people now saw that it was politic 'to become a Christian'. This soon degenerated into being the 'fashion' and an enormous shift occurred from the days of zealous and urgent commitment to the Great Commission. Perhaps for the first time since the days of John the Baptist, baptism and true discipleship became disassociated from each other. Consequently, for many people Christianity became a 'spectator sport' rather than a lifestyle of faith and obedience to Christ, particularly as large numbers now saw it to be financially attractive to become part of the 'paid clergy'. Meanwhile Constantine, desperate to have the church united no matter what the cost, imposed his own opinions on doctrinal discussion, which greatly affected the Council of Nicea in AD 325. Equally a link was made between Church and State, which set a pattern to the detriment of the gospel for centuries to come where, in some instances, mass baptisms and enforced conversion to Christianity became the order of the day. Added to this, the fourth century became littered with debate surrounding the question of the deity of Christ. What is clear is that when the Church seeks popularity or power, which by its very nature is inevitably transient, particularly when linked to the State, or has the use of unlimited financial resources, these things have generally proved to be the enemies of the Great Commission. History shows that they encourage misplaced trust and complacency, in addition to having the tendency to undermine the spiritual vitality of the people of God.

## I's dotted and T's crossed !

A respected church leader in Eastern Europe, when speaking with me recently, expressed a concern relating to a number of carefully selected national Christians they had sent to the UK over the last ten years with the purpose of studying theology. The objective was to see nationals equipped to teach and train others in their home country. The leader's comment was that, overall, it had been a disastrous experience. His assessment was that it had produced a group of theological 'academics' who returned home with more questions than answers and who were now bereft of any vision or zeal for ministry or mission. Even tempering these comments with the fact that they came from someone who had lived through the Communist days, where God's supernatural keeping and protecting power had to be known day-by-day compared to what is all too often our cold and spiritless Western approach to our faith, these are still very challenging observations. I would suggest that such comments are worthy of consideration, not so much as a statement on our theological training, although that in itself could be discussed, but rather as a reminder that the Lord urged his disciples to love him with *mind and heart*.

As I have attempted to show in the previous chapters, a sound understanding of biblical and doctrinal truth is of prime importance, but an interesting feature of the New Testament church was the speed with which new converts, with the minimum of training, became missionaries. Added to this, we see the apostle Paul adopting what today might be considered to be a 'high risk' approach to ministry, as he quickly moved on from newly-established local congregations, apparently leaving the work in the hands of those with relatively little teaching. Yes, of course, this gave rise to some problems which had to be further addressed, but overall, by God's grace, this did not hinder the spread of the gospel.

Following the spiritual darkness of the Middle Ages we ought always to thank God for the sixteenth-century Reformation and the consequential return to biblical truth, later spearheaded by the men that God raised up in the Puritan era. But, it is noticeable that for a number of very valid reasons neither of these periods appear to have produced any great emphasis concerning the mandate given in the Great Commission. One can appreciate that the Reformers and Puritans had many difficult and costly battles to fight in their own lands, often under extreme persecution; added to the fact that they had relatively little knowledge of the world beyond Europe.

It is always dangerous to generalize and some exceptions can be seen clearly. Calvin, for one, was intensely concerned to send missionaries and preachers into France and supported an attempt to establish mission in South America. But, while in principle Luther asserted and re-established the doctrine of the priesthood of all believers rather than ministry being in the hands of a few select, trained clerics, in practice, the Reformation seems not to have produced a great missionary emphasis or concern among the laity. Equally, the invaluable wealth of Bible teaching and doctrinal truth left to us by the Puritans did not produce great global missionary endeavour at that time. As evangelicals, we must be sure that, above all else, our love for the written word of God is always leading us to greater devotion and love of the one who is the Living Word — our Lord and Saviour, Jesus Christ. Truth is essential, but we recall that Jesus came 'full of grace and truth' (John 1:14). Maybe the apostle Paul's words to Timothy are the most helpful way to summarize the thoughts of this chapter, as appropriate to those who desire to serve God in these important and challenging times:

Timothy, guard what has been entrusted to your care...
But you, man of God ... pursue righteousness, godliness,

faith, love, endurance and gentleness. Fight the good fight of the faith. Take hold of the eternal life to which you were called when you made your good confession in the presence of many witnesses

(1 Timothy 6:20, 11-12).

## Questions to consider!

In terms of the subject matter discussed in this chapter, can you identify any current trends in evangelical thought or ministry that point us to believe that history is repeating itself?

In the light of the above question and as we consider the historical journey of the church of Jesus Christ, what practical lessons can we learn, 'to help guide our steps aright in the present' (as quoted from Renwick's *The Story of the Church* on page 111)?

# 10.
# Catching God's heartbeat

*We have greater work to do here than merely securing our own salvation. We are members of the world and Church, and we must labour to do good to many. We are trusted with our Master's talents for His service, in our places to do our best to propagate His truth, and grace, and Church, and to bring home souls, and honour His cause, and edify His flock, and further the salvation of as many as we can. All this is to be done on earth, if we will secure the end of all in heaven.*[1]

His disciples came to him and said, 'Explain to us the parable of the weeds in the field.' He answered, 'The one who sowed the good seed is the Son of Man. The field is the world, and the good seed stands for the sons of the kingdom'

(Matthew 13:36-37).

You will recall that the previous chapter mentioned how through persecution the believers of the New Testament church were scattered like seed throughout Judea, Samaria and eventually to the far reaches of the Roman Empire and how, in consequence, the church grew. Reference has been made to the brutal persecutions of some of the emperors, who eventually gave up their work of slaughter because the blood of the martyrs proved to be the seed of the church. Passing comment has recalled those whose life-giving sacrifice brought reformation to Europe, and how, in more recent days, contemporary Christians have held a firm witness to their faith, resulting in the subsequent spread of the gospel. In the context of this unfolding story, it is important to remind ourselves that, above all, Jesus is the Sower and that the entire history of the Great Commission being played out through the life of the church is the result of God sowing the 'sons of the kingdom' according to his sovereign purposes and not necessarily according to our plans or fancies.

In commenting on the Lord's words to the apostle Paul that as he had given testimony in Jerusalem, so he would in Rome (Acts 23:11), Spurgeon asks:

*Are you a witness for the Lord, and are you just now in danger? Then remember you are immortal till your work is done. If the Lord has more witness for you to bear, you will live to bear it.*[2]

It was in the light of such thinking that at the age of fifty-two C. T. Studd,[3] forced to return to England because of ill health after establishing a work in China, felt God's call to Africa. He had every reason to stay at home:

*…but an amusing notice in a Liverpool window, 'Cannibals want missionaries', drew his attention to the needs of Africa. He discovered that while traders, hunters and officials had ventured into the interior, there were areas where no Christians had taken the Gospel.*[4]

It was in this setting that C. T. Studd made the following memorable statement:

*If Jesus Christ be God and died for me, then no sacrifice can be too great for me to make for Him.*

and of such fibre are men and women of mission made.

## Sown in his field!

In the vine and branches illustration used by our Lord, he makes this clear statement, 'My Father is the gardener' (John 15:1). One can only feel that the great Sower went out with tears on some occasions, as he scattered his precious seed in the dark places of suffering and death. 'Sowing means, death, darkness and loneliness', writes F. B. Meyer.[5] He continues in the context of John 12:24-25:

*Unless an ear of wheat falls to the ground and dies, it remains only a single seed. But if it dies, it produces many seeds,*

and then remarks,

*we must be prepared to die, not only to sins, and weights, and self-indulgences, but to our own notions of pleasing God, to our emotional life, to our self-congratulation at the results of Christian service, to the energy and enthusiasm of our devotion.*

This reminds us again that only the one who is a true disciple, surrendered to the will and purposes of God, can hope to fulfil the demands of Christ's mandate to his church. David Haag, commenting on the Great Commission's call to the church, reminds us that 'Christ's most frequently repeated command in Scripture is not "receive me", but "follow me".'

Haag then coins the phrase 'self-serving service', pointing out that it is possible to seem to be serving Christ and others, when in reality we are only serving ourselves; whereas 'Christ-like service' always serves God.

He then gives what he considers to be the distinguishing marks of self-serving service, by which each of us can check ourselves.

1. *Those serving in this way generally have a constant need to be noticed. The greater the degree of visibility, the stronger the motivation to serve.*
2. *What appeals to them is usually the 'bigger the better' acts of service — tasks 'worthy' of their time and talents.*
3. *They are prone to render service for results.*
4. *Self–service is often shortsighted. So long as it is convenient and not too costly, it may be given.*[6]

Referring to the text in John 12:24 again, we see that the central theme of this message and the surrounding verses is the glory of God. Jesus uses the image of the seed to illustrate the great spiritual truth that just as there can be no victory without surrender, so there can be no fruit without death and no glory without suffering. In verse 23 of John 12, Jesus is speaking of his own death. He is aware that his Father is to sow him into Calvary's bed of suffering. At this time, one would expect the Lord to be saying, 'The hour has come for the Son of Man to be *crucified.*' However, the text records Christ's words to be, 'The hour has come for the Son of Man to be *glorified.*' In practice there is not only a bountiful harvest when a seed 'dies' but there is also a beautiful harvest. Above all, Christ shows the church that the only way to have a fruitful life is to follow him

in 'death', 'burial' and 'resurrection'. This is the life that will be
fruitful and glorify him.

If you were to meet David, he gives a lasting impression
of a man called of God to a pioneer work, totally surrendered
to the task entrusted to him and ably supported by his wife.
In Communist Romania he was successfully 'pastoring' a local
church. Following the Romanian revolution, David looked
forward to the expansion of God's work in his area, but for some
reason he could not feel at ease. He was aware that just across
the border in the Ukraine were Romanian-speaking villages
void of any gospel witness and this became a burden on his
heart. An initial exploratory visit led to a summer evangelistic
mission into several of these villages. Having the advantage
of a common Romanian language and culture, David and
the gospel message he brought found a ready response. Souls
were saved, yet there was no one to care for them. With the
promise of prayer and practical support from Romania, David
subsequently moved into one of the Ukrainian villages with his
family. Their new living conditions were far inferior to those
left behind in Romania and, with no financial support coming
for the first seven months, they lived on potatoes and bread.

During that time David and his wife frequently questioned
whether they had mistaken the Lord's calling. In material terms,
truly they had been 'sown' into a rocky and hard place. However,
the Lord graciously blessed their ministry and a growing local
church has been established. Today, a refurbished barn has
been converted into a lovely church building and incorporates
a comfortable flat for David and his family. Under his energetic
and caring leadership, this 'mother church' has planted two
other local congregations in nearby villages and other local
believers are being trained in leadership in order to expand the
ministry further.

*In a world of mediocrity and confusion, God calls you to excellence and discernment. There's the story of a pilot who came on the loudspeaker mid-flight and said, 'I have some good news and some bad news. The bad news is, we've lost all our instrumentation and I don't know where we are. The good news is, we have a strong tail wind and are making great time.' That's an accurate picture of how many people live: they have no direction in life, but they're getting there fast! As Christians, we are to be different because we have divine guidance and eternal goals. Our lives are to be marked by a confident trust in God and a pursuit of excellence.[7]*

If we believe these things to be true, the big question is how can such truths be 'earthed' into our everyday lives, both as individuals and as members of local congregations?

## Some current comments

During the latter part of 2003 I conducted a 'straw poll'[8] among pastors and church leaders drawn from a cross-section of local churches in the UK. This was in the form of a questionnaire submitted to local church leaders, with their consent. The spread was across the denominations with all of the churches having a conservative evangelical emphasis and known to have an active concern and involvement in 'mission'. The churches varied in membership from up to fifty to two hundred plus and in answering the questionnaire the pastors were asked to consider 'mission' in its broadest sense; that is, in terms of ministry both at home and abroad. The aim of the exercise was to acquire some current, objective comment from the frontline of local church life with regard to the thinking on 'mission' and the challenges this brings.

- All the churches had either a missionary leadership and/ or a mission board drawn from their lay members. They had the responsibility of overseeing mission concern and involvement. 40% of the churches found it helpful to have a 'Mission Statement' in addition to their 'Statement of Faith'. In these cases it appeared that the desire was to emphasize that 'mission' lies at the heart of the church and ought not to be considered as an addition or optional extra.

- 85% of the churches had members involved in 'full-time ministry', serving in a mission context. The number tended to be proportionate to the size of the membership. Of those in 'full-time ministry', there was a 50% split between those who were serving in the UK and those serving overseas and almost all were ministering through the auspices of mission agencies/societies.

- Although there was no direct question to this effect, a number mentioned their financial commitment to 'mission' as a proportion of their church's income. This varied between 15% - 45%.

- A question concerning the extent of *regular* contact with mission agencies revealed that most rationalized to an average of six or seven per church, although one church had contact with only one mission and another with twelve different missions. The proportionate spread of interest resulted in 35% of the contact being with UK ministries and 65% with overseas work.

- In relation to contacts with mission agencies by the local church, a question was asked whether this was proving to be:

a. Very helpful; b. Helpful; c. Both positive and negative; d. Unhelpful.

60% responded that the contacts had been very helpful,
20% — helpful
20% — both positive and negative

• When asked what was proving to be the most effective 'mission' stimulus to the church all, without exception, highlighted the importance of exposure through visiting speakers and/or meetings conducted by those from within the church, giving first-hand reports. Additionally, 20% underlined the stimulus created by prayer involvement and 30% found that biblical teaching and preaching concerning 'mission' was essential to stimulate the church.

• Conversely, a question was posed asking what was found to work against engendering and maintaining a mission concern within the local church. 90% responded by suggesting that through various reasons, lack of time and commitment to the life and ministry of the local church by members and adherents also showed itself in lack of mission interest and concern.

  Other responses drew attention to negative reactions by the church because of:
  a. poor presentation by the mission agency and/or its representative, often accompanied by a lack of specific focus — 40% response
  b. an information overload by the mission agency — 20% response
  c. a lack of a sound biblical base by the mission agency — 10% response

- Questioned concerning the benefits or otherwise to the local church of involvement in 'short-term service' by members of the church, all felt that the first-hand exposure to frontline ministry encouraged, challenged and brought blessing to the local church as a whole.

  30% suggested that 'short-term ministry' had been beneficial in testing the gifts and callings of some of their members.

  40% saw the danger of 'short-term ministry' as inculcating a 'short-term' ethos and thinking, rather than the life commitment that is needed in both local church life and in mission.

  40% drew attention to the fact that 'short-term ministry' unfortunately gave an avenue for those who were simply looking for an 'adventurous break' or a 'time-out' experience.

- One final question asked the local church leaders to complete the following sentence. 'I wish that mission agencies would understand that...'

- Almost without exception there was a heartfelt request that mission agencies would understand that the local church is the sending agency — some added, 'and not simply a funding source'. There was a significant request that, in these days, mission agencies should have an absolutely clear, biblical, purpose statement.

  Additionally, a plea was made that mission agencies would liaise more with the life and programme of the local church and take positive measures to train their representatives in communicating their message in a relevant and succinct manner in both presentation and written reports/prayer letters.

If the above findings can be considered to be exemplifying the current situation in our local churches in the UK, there appear to be lessons for everyone to take on board.

## What place — the mission agency?

It is clear that although a great deal of ground has been made up by mission agencies over recent years, in recognizing the essential, biblical role of the local church as the sending source of mission and mission workers, obviously churches continue to feel that there is a shortfall in this area. If we believe that mission agencies still have a role to play, they should readily acknowledge that, at best, they are para-church organizations. Yet, even as such, they can fulfil a vital role as the servant of both the local and universal church.

Our Lord set the pattern when he said to the disciples, as they argued who would be the greatest, 'But I am among you as one who serves' (Luke 22:27). Notice that the word 'serves' used here has its root in '*diakonia*', relating to the one who serves everyone else at the table. The 'servant heart' seems to be such a rare commodity in Christian circles today. How wonderful if mission agencies would set the example by liaising with local churches as a servant, to assist them in fulfilling their mission concern, rather than simply always asking them to fall in with the mission's programme! Who knows, maybe this would even help in addressing the 'empire building' mentality that has been all too apparent in some aspects of missionary endeavour.

With a little more forethought this servant-role can be extended even further. In 1989 Larry Pate gathered data relating to the Third World churches and their involvement in global mission. From this he was able to show that 'a large part of the future of mission was proving to belong to the missionaries of Latin America, Africa, Asia and Oceania'.[9] This reminds us that whilst there has been a noticeable decline in the strength and influence of the Christian church in Western European countries and North America, many other parts of the world have been seeing a significant movement of God, resulting in substantial church growth and witness.

Where missions are working in such areas, this presents them with a great opportunity to take an intermediary role. Our tendency is to think of overseas mission as simply 'from us to them', but in bringing to the UK churches the testimony of those places where God is particularly blessing the work of the gospel, the mission agency can fulfil an important, and often much needed, ministry of encouragement and challenge.

Additionally, it is significant that the straw poll revealed a desire by local churches to see mission agencies clearly stating their theological stance. We live in days when words like 'evangelical' and 'born again' carry with them a whole variety of concepts and meanings. Where once 'ecumenical' was understood to mean inter-denominational, in some Christian circles this word has been hijacked to portray a 'multi-faith' stance. Small wonder that local churches need some assurance concerning those with whom they are linking arms. The reality is that we are fast reaching a position where it is almost as important to state, not simply what we believe, but also what we do not believe. I suggest that mission agencies should be addressing this matter carefully.

## What place — the local church?

Question! Has the task of missionary education in our local churches been left in the hands of visiting speakers in 'deputation meetings' and 'missionary weekends' far too much?

It cannot be without significance that only 30% of the churches contacted in the straw poll made reference to Bible preaching and teaching as a stimulus to mission concern, and only 20% to that of prayer involvement. In contrast, great store was placed upon the 'first-hand experience' and/or reports by those directly involved. As Samuel Escobar reminds us:

> In fact the Bible was instrumental in reforming the sixteenth–
> century church in two dimensions: (i) evangelizing people
> who were only nominal Christians; and (ii) renewing genuine
> Christians spiritually and morally, who were now enabled to
> face the challenge of the modern era opening at that historical
> moment.[10]

Continuing to speak of the development of the Moravian movement leading to the missionary work of the nineteenth and twentieth centuries, Escobar goes on to assert:

> During that time Protestant missions achieved one of the most
> extensive advances in missionary history, and the Bible played a
> pivotal role in it.

In days when the 'touchy-feely' ethos of postmodernism has been allowed to penetrate deeply into Christian thought, have we compromised, or even sacrificed, our belief in the power of God's Word to convict and convince our hearts?

Another factor which has worked against an over-reliance on the deputation meeting is the occasion when the visiting speaker was a missionary on furlough, and was undoubtedly an excellent servant of God in his own field of ministry overseas, but was not a 'platform person' or the type of charismatic figure who enthused others, leaving the inevitable negative reaction. Personally I have always had serious reservations with regard to the 'annual missionary weekend' approach, where this is looked upon as the great stimulus to the local church's missionary concern. Is it advisable to put three missionaries on the same platform with their 'fifteen minutes each' of reporting time? Or conversely, is it reasonable to expect the church to absorb a barrage of information from three, four or more missions over three days of intensive missionary sessions, when at the end it is difficult to recall who said what, about where?

Of course, exposure to what God is doing, by hearing and seeing what is happening beyond our small corner, will always have its place and ought to enlarge our missionary vision, but unless we are motivated by love for Christ and his word, even this will accomplish little of eternal value. Far better for all concerned if the visitor can be used as part of the overall teaching and education of the church in mission, through which the church is brought to the point reached by the apostle Paul as he exclaimed:

For Christ's love compels us, because we are convinced that one died for all, and therefore all died. And he died for all, that those who live should no longer live for themselves but for him who died for them and was raised again

(2 Corinthians 5:14-15).

## Two 'very great and precious promises'

1. 'And I tell you … on this rock I will build my church, and
   the gates of Hades will not overcome it'

   (Matthew 16:18).

Matthew 16 records how Jesus has taken his disciples to the northern region of Caesarea Philippi where the snow-capped Mount Hermon portrayed a beauty and serenity all of its own. Jesus is beginning to tell them clearly that his imminent death is not only a certainty, but also a necessity. Now, our Lord seeks to put into the hearts of the disciples those essential truths that will be important for them when he has returned to the Father. So it is, that through Peter, he draws from them the great confession that 'You are the Christ, the Son of the living God'. This in turn leads to the Saviour giving the encouraging promise that he will build his church.

Notice two important aspects concerning this promise.

### a. *It is a promise that is unconditional.*

One would have expected the Lord to have said, 'If you are faithful, I will build my church.' After all, they were the ones he had called and trained to tell out the message of the gospel. How blessed we are to know that ultimately the building of the church is dependent upon Christ and his word and not upon his disciples who, like us, were prone to deny, betray and desert their Master. This gives us no excuse to be lax or indifferent in the work of mission. On the contrary, it encourages us more than ever to know the joy of being part of what God is doing.

**b.** *It is a promise built upon a firm foundation.*

Theologians have long debated the reference to 'the rock' upon which the church is built. If we set this reference in the context of the preceding verses, we note the specific way in which Jesus addresses Peter. In calling him Simon, son of Jonah, the word of God draws our attention to the fact that Peter is no more than a sinful man, born of man, and as such has no innate spiritual understanding. In fact, he is like all men, by nature, 'dead in trespasses and sins'. Peter has nothing within himself that leads him to the great spiritual truth that Jesus is the Christ, the Son of the living God. It is only because 'my Father in heaven has revealed this to you' that he comes to understand this incredible and eternal truth.

Then our Lord says, 'and I tell you that you are Peter, and on this rock I will build my church'. I would suggest that it is God's revelation of gospel truth to sinful man that is the rock, the foundation, on which the church has been, and will be, built. This should come again as an encouragement to all who would engage in mission. What blessing this brings! We have the assurance that a merciful and gracious God will not only build his church according to his promise, but we see how he will build his church, as he works the miracle of quickening the hearts of sinful men to redeem them to himself!

2. 'And surely I am with you always, to the very end of the age'

(Matthew 28:20).

Matthew, re-echoing the prophecy of Isaiah 7:14, records in chapter one, verse 23, that Jesus was to be born as '"Immanuel

— which means, "God with us"'. Matthew 18:20 finds Jesus assuring his followers that as they '...come together in my name, there am I with them'.

Now, in the concluding sentence of his Gospel, Matthew again draws our attention to the certainty of Christ's presence among his people, as they engage in mission.

These statements rest on the truth that it is Jehovah, God, who is with his people in every circumstance and for all time, until history comes to its foreordained conclusion. Consequently, he will impart direction, wisdom, strength, encouragement and consolation as, and when, it is needed. This gives the glorious possibility for every one of us as disciples of Jesus Christ to see the Great Commission fulfilled through our lives and ministry, whatever that ministry might be. Campbell Morgan writes:

> *Many years ago I was sitting by the side of an aged saint of God, an old woman of eighty-five. I had been reading Matthew chapter twenty-eight to her and when I finished at verse twenty, I looked at her and said, 'This is a great promise.'* She looked up and said sharply, with the light of sanctified humour in her eyes: 'That is not a promise at all, that is a fact.' *Oh, if only the Church of God could remember that fact!*[11]

## And finally...

As every preacher knows, when he says 'finally', then he should finish. Therefore to do this and in order to 'earth' the principles which have been discussed into the practicalities of local church and mission life, I ask that you pause and consider prayerfully the following concluding questions.

1. What is the most important principle, concept or lesson God has laid on my heart, as I have read through these pages?

2. Considering that which I have identified from the question above, what is the next action that I need to take to implement this into:
   a. my personal life;
   b. my local church life;
   c. my work, contact or association with mission agencies?

3. Are there other subsidiary principles, which have caught my attention and which need my further consideration and/or application?

# Notes

## Chapter 1

1. Goldsmith, *Don't just stand there*, IVP, 1976, p.7.
2. Millar, *Outgrowing the Ingrown Church,* Zondervan, 1986.
3. Tozer, *Christ, the Eternal Son*, STL Books, 1982, p.81.

## Chapter 2

1. Peskott and Ramachandra, *The Message of Mission*, IVP, 2003, p.108.
2. Costas, *The Church and its Mission*, Tyndale House, 1974, p.135.

## Chapter 3

1. Tozer, *Christ the Eternal Son*, STL Books, 1982, p.140.
2. Dr M. Lloyd-Jones, *The Kingdom of God*, Crossways Books, 1992, p.207.

## Chapter 4

1. Bavinck, *An introduction to the Science of Missions,* Presbyterian and Reformed Publishing Co., 1960, p.11.
2. As above, p.14.
3. Gibbs, *I believe in Church Growth*, Hodder and Stoughton, 1981, p.39.

## Chapter 5

1. Pink, *The Divine inspiration of the Bible*, Guardian Press, 1976, p.65.
2. Gibbs, *Church Growth*, p. 26.
3. Wiersbe, *Real Worship*, Kingsway Publications, 1986, p.97.
4. Negrut, *Glimpses of God's Grace,* Slavic Gospel Association, 2001, appraisal comment on rear cover.
5. Hendriksen, *New Testament Commentary — John,* Banner of Truth, 1982, p.361.

## Chapter 6

1. Broadbent, *The Pilgrim Church*, The Evangelical Heritage Series, Marshall Pickering, 1989, p.123.
2. Jackman, *Understanding the Church*, Mentor, 1996, p.187.
3. Halcombe, as told by Hristo Kulichev, *Imprisoned for Christ*, Tyndale House Publishers Inc., 2001.
4. Dr John Killinger, President of the Mission for Biblical Literacy.

## Chapter 7

1. Jackman, *Understanding the Church*, p.22.
2. Oden, *After Modernity ....What?,* Academic Books, 1990.
3. Allen, *Christian belief in a Post-modern World*, Westminster/John Knox Press, 1989, p.3.
4. Johnston, *Preaching to a Post-modern World,* IVP, 2001, p.26.
5. Harvey, *The Condition of Post-Modernity: An Enquiry into the Origins of Cultural Change,* MIT Press, 1987, p.43.
6. Kenneth Gergen, *The Saturated Sel,* Basic Books, 1991.
7. Middleton and Walsh, *Truth is stranger than it used to be,* IVP, 1995, p.58.
8. Stott, *Issues Facing Christians Today,* Marshall Pickering, 1990, p.67.

9. Iain Murray, *D. Martyn Lloyd-Jones — The First Forty Years*, Banner of Truth, 1982, p.94.

10. Millar, *Marketplace Preaching: How to Return the Sermon to Where it Belongs*, Baker, 1995, p.134.

11. Wayne Grudem, *Systematic Theology*, IVP/Zondervan, 1994, p.483.

12. Philip P. Bliss (1838-76).

13. Bavinck, *An introduction to the Science of Missions*, Presbyterian & Reformed Publishing, 1960, pp.108-9.

## Chapter 8

1. MacArthur, *Ashamed of the Gospel*, Crossways Books, 1993, p.xvi.

2. Hughes, *Liberating Ministry from the Success Syndrome*, Tyndale, 1987, p.9.

3. Wilson, *Wilson's Old Testament Word Studies*, MacDonald Publishing Co., pp.159-60.

4. The Bible word frequently translated 'servant' is the Greek '*doulos*' — a slave. It is a 'strong' word conveying total servitude to the master in that the slave had no rights or future of his own, outside of his master's will.

5. Mallard, *F.I.E.C. Together magazine*, Autumn 2003, lead article.

6. MacArthur, *Ashamed of the Gospel*, Crossway Books, 1993, p.97.

7. Edwards, *The Wrath of Almighty God — God's Judgement Against Sinners*, Soli Deo Gloria Publications, p.347.

8. Peskett & Ramchandra, *The Message of Mission*, IVP, 2003, p.239ff.

## Chapter 9

1. As told by Kulichev to Halcombe, *Imprisoned for Christ*, Tyndale House Publishers, Inc., 2001, pp.96,97,98.

2. *Glasnost* — openness.

3. *Perestroika* — reconstruction.

4. Renwick, *The Story of the Church*, IVP, first published in 1958, p.8.

5. For example, the writings of Eusebius of Nicomedia, Tactius the Roman historian, and Tertullian the Montanist.

6. As quoted in Samuel Green's *A Handbook of Church History*, The Religious Tract Society, 1904, p.55.

7. As above.

8. Peskett & Ramachandra, *The Message of Mission*, IVP, 2003, p.197.

9. It is important to note here that the term in the original — *Christ's afflictions* — is never used by any of the New Testament writers in respect to Christ's redemptive suffering associated with the cross whereby God's righteous judgement was fully met. As Matthew Poole remarks: '...nothing will be required from any believer on that account … all was filled up by Christ Himself' (John 19:30; Romans 6:9-10; Hebrews 10:14). See Matthew Poole's *Commentary on the Holy Bible*, Banner of Truth, 1969, p.712.

10. Broadbent, *The Pilgrim Church*, Marshall Pickering (The Evangelical Heritage Series), 1989, p.29.

11. Extracted from *Moving God's Finger*, Harris, Slavic Gospel Association Publication, 1991, pp.45, 46.

12. Pelagius appears to have been a British monk and although he was a man of ascetic habits and blameless life he denied the doctrine of original sin and refused to believe that the sinner was helpless to save himself. He was the centre of the Pelegian Controversy in 412 & 415 in Synods at Carthage and Bethlehem respectively.

13. Eusebius' *Ecclesiastical History*.

## Chapter 10

1. Richard Baxter as quoted in *A Puritan Golden Treasury*, Banner of Truth, 1977, p.93.

2. C. H. Spurgeon, *Cheque Book of the Bank of Faith Daily Readings*, Christian Focus Publications, 1996, p.99.

3. Charlie (or C T) Studd (1862-1931) was one of three brothers born to Edward Studd, a retired planter from India. CT became one of England's greatest all-round cricketers and played in Australia with the MCC team, which recovered the 'Ashes' during the winter tour of 1882-83. Soundly converted in 1875 he felt the call of God to China and was accepted as an associate member of the China Inland Mission under Hudson Taylor. On his twenty-fifth birthday CT came into a large inheritance that he promptly donated to various aspects of the Lord's work, leaving himself and his wife Priscilla virtually penniless as they went out to serve the Lord in China. The classic biography of CT Studd, as founder of what is today W.E.C. International, was written by Norman P. Grubb, entitled *C.T. Studd, Cricketer & Pioneer* and first published in 1933.

4. Hanks, *70 Great Christians Changing the World*, Christian Focus Publications, 2003, p.213.

5. F. B. Meyer, *The Prophet of Hope: Studies in Zechariah,* Ambassador, 1995, pp.90-91.

6. David Haag, *Living to Please God,* Christian Focus Publications, 1992, p.142.

7. John MacArthur, *Drawing Near: Daily Readings,* Crossways Books, 1993, reading for 20 February.

8. As this was not intended to be an extensive exercise, where percentage figures are given in the findings, they are rounded off to the nearest 5%. The aim of the exercise was to acquire some current, objective comment from the frontline of local

church life with regard to the thinking on 'mission' and the challenges this brings.

9. Pate, *From Every People,* MARC, 1989, p.5.

10. Escobar, A *Time for Mission – The Challenge of Global Christianity,* IVP, 2003, p.132.

11. Campbell Morgan, *The Gospel According to Matthew,* Marshall, Morgan and Scott, 1976, p.321.

# Bibliography

Allen, D. *Christian Belief in a Postmodern World*, Westminster/John Knox Press, 1989.

Bavinck, J. H. *An introduction to the Science of Missions*, The Presbyterian and Reformed Publishing Company, 1966.

Baxter, R. As quoted in *A Puritan Golden Treasury*, Banner of Truth, 1977.

Broadbent, E. H. *The Pilgrim Church*, Marshall Pickering — The Evangelical Heritage Series, 1989.

Costas, O. *The Church and its Mission*, Tyndale House, 1974.

Edwards, J. *The Wrath of Almighty God — God's Judgment Against Sinners*, Soli Deo Gloria Publications.

Escobar, S. *A Time for Mission*, IVP, 2003.

Gergen, K. *The Saturated Self*, Basic Books, 1989.

Goldsmith, M. *Don't Just Stand There!*, IVP, 1976.

Green, S. *A Handbook of Church History*, The Religious Tract Society, 1904.

Grudem, W. *Systematic Theology*, IVP/Zondervan, 1994.

Haag, D. *Living to Please God,* Christian Focus Publications Ltd, 1992.

Hanks, G. *70 Great Christians Changing the World,* Christian Focus Publications, 2003 ed.

Harris, T. *Moving God's Finger,* Slavic Gospel Association, 1991.

Harvey, D. *The Condition of Post Modernity — An enquiry into the Origins of Culture Change,* MIT Press, 1987.

Hendriksen, W. *New Testament Commentary — John,* Banner of Truth, 1982.

Hughes, K. *Liberating Ministry from the Success Syndrome,* Tyndale, 1987.


Jackman, D. *Understanding the Church,* Mentor, 1996.

Johnson, G. *Preaching to a Postmodern World,* IVP, 2001.


Kulichev, H. by Halcombe. *Imprisoned for Christ,* Tyndale, 2001.


Lloyd-Jones, M. *The Kingdom of God,* Crossways Books, 1992.


MacArthur, J. *Ashamed of the Gospel,* Crossways Books, 1993.
    *Drawing Near – Daily Readings,* Crossways Books, 1993.

Meyer, F. B. *The Prophet of Hope: Studies in Zechariah,* Ambassador, 1995.

Middleton and Walsh. *Truth is Stranger Than it Used to Be,* IVP, 1995.

Millar, C. *Marketplace Preaching, How to Return the Sermon to Where it Belongs,* Baker, 1995.

Millar, J. C. *Outgrowing the Ingrown Church,* Zondervan, 1986.

Morgan, G. C. *The Gospel According to Matthew,* Marshall, Morgan and Scott, 1976.

Murray, I. *Dr M. Lloyd-Jones, The First Forty Years,* Banner of Truth, 1982.

Oden, T. *After Modernity — What?*, Academic Books, 1990.

Otter, J. *The Witness of Czech Protestantism*, Prague — Kalich, 1970.

Pate, L. *From Every Place*, MARC, 1989.

Peskett and Ramachandra, *The Message of Mission*, IVP, 2003.

Peters. *Biblical Theology of Missions*, Moody Press, 1972.

Pink, A. *The Divine Inspiration of the Bible*, Guardian Press, 1976.

Poole, M. *Commentary on the Holy Bible*, Banner of Truth, 1982.

Renwick, A. M. *The Story of the Church*, IVP, 1953.

Slavic Gospel Association. *Glimpses of God's Grace*, S.G.A. Publication, 2001.

Spurgeon, C. H. *Cheque Book of the Bank of Faith Daily Readings*, Christian Focus Publications, 1996 edition.

Stott, J. *Issues Facing Christians Today*, Marshall Pickering, 1990.

Tozer, A. W. *Christ, the Eternal Son*, STL Books, 1982.

Wiersbe, W. *Real Worship*, Kingsway Publications, 1986.

Wilson, W. *Wilson's Old Testament Word Studies*, MacDonald Publishing Company.

# Scripture index

A wide range of excellent books on spiritual subjects is available from Evangelical Press. Please write to us for your free catalogue or contact us by e-mail.

Evangelical Press
Faverdale North Industrial Estate, Darlington, DL3 0PH, England

Evangelical Press USA
P. O. Box 825, Webster, New York 14580, USA

E-mail: sales@evangelicalpress.org
Web: www.evangelicalpress.org